Restoring God
BROKEN PEOPLE CAN BE REMADE *by* the RESTORING GOD

BRIAN GOODWIN

WESTBOW
PRESS®
A DIVISION OF THOMAS NELSON
& ZONDERVAN

Copyright © 2023 Brian Goodwin.

All rights reserved. No part of this book may be used or reproduced by any means, graphic, electronic, or mechanical, including photocopying, recording, taping or by any information storage retrieval system without the written permission of the author except in the case of brief quotations embodied in critical articles and reviews.

This book is a work of non-fiction. Unless otherwise noted, the author and the publisher make no explicit guarantees as to the accuracy of the information contained in this book and in some cases, names of people and places have been altered to protect their privacy.

WestBow Press books may be ordered through booksellers or by contacting:

WestBow Press
A Division of Thomas Nelson & Zondervan
1663 Liberty Drive
Bloomington, IN 47403
www.westbowpress.com
844-714-3454

Because of the dynamic nature of the Internet, any web addresses or links contained in this book may have changed since publication and may no longer be valid. The views expressed in this work are solely those of the author and do not necessarily reflect the views of the publisher, and the publisher hereby disclaims any responsibility for them.

Any people depicted in stock imagery provided by Getty Images are models, and such images are being used for illustrative purposes only.
Certain stock imagery © Getty Images.

Unless otherwise indicated, all Scripture quotations are taken from the Holy Bible, NEW INTERNATIONAL VERSION®, NIV® Copyright © 1973, 1978, 1984, 2011 by Biblica, Inc.® Used by permission. All rights reserved worldwide.

Scripture quotations marked (ESV) are from the ESV® Bible (The Holy Bible, English Standard Version®), copyright © 2001 by Crossway, a publishing ministry of Good News Publishers. Used by permission. All rights reserved.

ISBN: 979-8-3850-1383-8 (sc)
ISBN: 979-8-3850-1384-5 (hc)
ISBN: 979-8-3850-1385-2 (e)

Library of Congress Control Number: 2023923126

Print information available on the last page.

WestBow Press rev. date: 12/18/2023

To my Lord and Savior, Jesus Christ. Without Your love and forgiveness, my life would not be the same. Your Spirit has helped this book come together from conception to writing to publishing. All the glory and honor for this book goes to You.

Contents

Chapter 1 Hope for the Broken... 1
    Earthquakes... 1
    Purpose of Restoring God 3
    The Restoration Manual 5
    All Glory to God... 6

Chapter 2 Ingredients of Life.. 9
    Faith 9
    Ingredients of a Recipe 13
    Joseph... 19
    Joseph Mixed with My Experience 22

Chapter 3 Holding on (to the Wrong Stuff) 26
    Truth 26
    The Pain in Life.. 29
    Israelites and Judges 33
    Truth Breaks the Cycle 35

Chapter 4 Drowning 40
    Guidance.. 40
    Losing My Way 42
    Samson 45
    Guidance Helps Prevent Losing Your Way 48

Chapter 5 Fallen 52
    Sin 52
    Sin Leads to Tragedy 54

    David and Uriah's Wife 56
    Letting Sin Rule 59

Chapter 6 Double Living 64
    Guilt and Shame 64
    Living with a Secret 69
    Peter and His Denials of Jesus 71
    Breaking Free 74

Chapter 7 Welcome to the Valley 78
    Provision 78
    Entering the Wilderness 81
    Israelites and the Exodus 84
    God's Provision Was a Wilderness 87

Chapter 8 The Fallout 92
    Discipline 92
    Discipline across Life Changes 96
    Job 100
    Discipline Leads to Renewed Hope 103

Chapter 9 Living in the Unknown 108
    Hope 108
    Questions without Answers 112
    Ruth 114
    Hope in the Unknown 116

Chapter 10 Making Lemonade 120
    Patience 120
    Patience on the Path 124
    Nehemiah and Jerusalem Rebuild 126
    Patience in the Wilderness of Life 130

Chapter 11 Almost to the Bottom 134
    Perseverance 134

Purposeful Persevering 137
　　Murderer Moses 140
　　Identity Matters 143

Chapter 12 Camp 146
　　Worship 146
　　Camp 149
　　Peter and Paul in Prison 151
　　Worship Moves God 153

Chapter 13 Release 156
　　Freedom 156
　　Released to Live Free 159
　　Prodigal Son 161
　　Freedom through Grace 162

Chapter 14 The Greater Restoration 166
　　Grace 166
　　Beautifully Remade 170
　　Jesus's Death and Resurrection 173

References 181

Introduction

KINTSUGI

> My sacrifice, O God, is a broken spirit; a broken and contrite heart you, God, will not despise.
> —Psalm 51:17

Kintsugi (*kint-soo-gee*) is a beautiful Japanese art form that exemplifies the power of restoration. It shows that broken things can be made useful again—that broken things need not stay broken. *Kintsugi* means golden (kin) repairing (tsugi). The art form is used to repair ceramic pottery and glass. It is an extension of the Japanese philosophy of wabi-sabi, which sees beauty in the incomplete and value in simplicity.[1]

Accidents happen, and pottery gets broken. Often, broken things are simply discarded in society, and new things are bought. However, this is not so with kintsugi. Kintsugi sees the broken pieces and sets out to mend and restore them. Using the sap from an indigenous Japanese tree as glue and molten precious metals such as gold, they fill the cracks, and pieces are bound together again. All this can take days, weeks, or even months to complete. Perhaps the most beautiful part of kintsugi is that the cracks are not hidden when the piece is mended. Instead, the broken lines are highlighted with gold. A finished restoration will prominently show the cracks as a focal point.

The meaning behind the art form is staggering. In kintsugi, the original pottery is seen as a beautiful piece with incredible potential.

It is purposeful and useful. However, the truth in life is that mistakes, accidents, and missteps happen. This includes wrongly motivated actions, which cause great damage. As a result, things can be rendered broken. In kintsugi, this does not mean that they are no longer useful. Kintsugi sees the broken pieces as integral parts of what makes the vessel beautiful. That is why the cracks are highlighted. They are made the focus of what is seen because the beauty of the restoration is in the mending of the brokenness.

Kintsugi is a powerful metaphor for human life. Broken lives can be remade and purposeful once again. In the process of restoring, the person sees how the brokenness has made them who they are and embraces the flaws and the pain. It does not hide it or try to cover it. Instead, the marks are put on display. The power of the art form is in how it emphasizes the beauty of human fragility. Kintsugi is a reminder to stay optimistic when things fall apart and to celebrate the flaws and missteps of life. It is an art form that encourages a person to learn that accepting and celebrating one's scars is a powerful lesson for life.[1] It is a lengthy process that builds strength and resilience and takes pride in the imperfect.

Psalm 51:17 says, "My sacrifice, O God, is a broken spirit; a broken and contrite heart you, God, will not despise." There are no sacrifices so dear to God as broken spirits. There are no offerings so precious to Him as contrite hearts. It would be impossible to conceive the power of restorations that have resulted because sinful people have turned from their corruption and have accepted Jesus's love that leads them back into God's forgiveness and favor. Do not be content with forgiveness. Seek restoration to a renewed life and then strive for better.[2]

I became aware of kintsugi one day while researching how best to fix the handle of a broken mug. As I read about the history of this art form, my mind was blown away. It was such a picture of what my life had experienced. It was a picture of what I want to communicate with you, the reader. Broken things do not have to stay broken. There is hope for restoration that involves a beautiful process of healing. God is the artist, and there is nothing that the Restoring God cannot restore.

Chapter 1
HOPE FOR THE BROKEN

> He will wipe away every tear from their eyes. There will be nor more death or mourning or crying or pain, for the old order of things has passed away.
> —Revelation 21:4

EARTHQUAKES

There is a digital picture frame on my desk that reminds me that life is a series of events and experiences. It is a representation of my life in many ways. Most of the images are from events that are positive and memorable. We love these events in our lives—birthdays, anniversaries, vacations, and holidays—that fill our photo albums and picture frames with positive memories. Some images remind me of events that led to healthy growth and taught valuable life lessons. I participated in a music group throughout high school, which taught me many lessons that grew my faith, musical knowledge, and personal maturity. Some images remind me of experiences that built character and guided me to become a better person. I had a job that went through a season of extended hours and unexpected calls for help day and night. It was not fun by any means, but it developed character in me, and I became a better person by persevering through it.

Then, there are some events that fall into a whole different category.

Images from these events do not make picture frames or albums. These events are like earthquakes in your life. These are the "rock your world" types of experiences that leave you shattered. These are events that damage and cause pain that you did not ask for and would not wish on anyone. Some earthquakes come about by way of other people, perhaps through a death or a broken relationship or a result of some other hardship. Other times, you may be the source of the earthquake that grieves others and inflicts pain in a way that affects many people because of your choices. All these earthquake events may lead you to brokenness. It takes you to the "valley of the shadow of death," as spoken of in Psalm 23. Have you been there? Perhaps you know of someone who has been there.

Life is different in the valley. When you are in that valley, you may be consumed with many questions, and most of them cannot be immediately answered. Where do you go from here? How do you navigate this valley? How can you get back or fix the scenario? What is needed to heal this wound? You want the pain to end. You want things back to the way they used to be (in some cases). You want it back to normal, but that is not possible because the person you were before no longer exists. There *will* be a new normal. Perhaps your best friend died, and you will not be able to talk to them again. Your house was destroyed by a tornado and is in pieces and unlivable. Your abusive husband is paying the price in lockup, and you are the one left to pick up the pieces. Or perhaps you are the perpetrator of the offense and must deal with the consequences of your actions. On either side of the coin, your relationships will be different. The damage is done. Repairs might be made, but things will never be the same.

> **Earthquakes change lives!**

If you were the perpetrator of an offense, you may not have any control over the consequences. How will you deal with not being in control? How will you respond to the looks and judgmental thoughts that people will have toward you? Earthquakes change lives!

Ultimately, what every person needs after these life-shifting earthquake events is restoration. Amid all the questions and confusion, a person needs to know that life will go on and there is hope for the future. The person mourning the loss of a spouse needs to grieve and have an outlet for their pain. Then, they, in time, will desire to be restored and receive love from another. The person affected by another person's physical mistreatment needs to be protected and nursed back to health. Then, they, in time, will desire to be restored to people who can offer healthy relationships. The offender needs to own their mistakes and seek to better themselves so that they will never offend again. Then, they, in time and when appropriate, will seek restoration with the people they love. Restoration is ultimately the goal. Restoration is what we all want deep down.

PURPOSE OF RESTORING GOD

Broken things do not need to stay broken. For those who have been broken, have experienced the valley, and who desire restoration, this book is written with you in mind. No one wants to stay broken. We want more from life, and I want to tell you that there *is* more. You can get to more. But more will mean less—less of your desires and more of God's desires. This is a process, but the process can lead to healing. Much of our brokenness comes from too much focus on ourselves. This was my story and the story of many restored people whom I have come to know. Restoration involves becoming more selfless.

God *is able* to restore that which is broken. That is who God is, a restorer. That is what this book is about. It is a book proclaiming that broken people are not useless. There *is* hope for the broken. Broken people need mending and healing, and there is a process to achieve that. This book guides and points the restoration seeker toward finding hope in the author of restoration.

Each chapter of this book contains three sections. First, each chapter describes the critical components needed for restoration. These are elements such as faith, hope, love, truth, patience, perseverance, and many more. We will look inwardly at how these elements play out in our minds and in our lives.

Second, the chapters tell my personal story of restoration. I tell how my selfish focus caused pain and anguish in others. I share how my choices caused the very people I loved to be hurt. Yet through a life refocused on Jesus, I came to experience a restored life.

Third, each chapter tells of a biblical story of restoration—stories that tell of an earthquake event that happened in the life of a character or group and their journey to restoration. In these stories, the God of the Bible shows that not only is He proficient at restoring broken people, but that He also uses them to do mighty things.

What is restoration? Restoration involves revival through repair. This is the essence of kintsugi mentioned in the preface.

The revival piece is achieved by reidentifying who we are. It is finding the true identity of who we are through the one who created us with purpose. This often takes us through a redefining of our lives' governing values. As a kid, every October 31, I donned a costume and tried to look like someone else. But that person I tried to look like was not who I really was. Many people today go through life trying to be someone they really are not. They mask their identities, trying to impress others or live an illusionary life of who they think they really want to be. But that identity is often different from the identity that Jesus calls us to. He calls us away from a self-focused identity to a God-enabled identity for the times and conditions for which He has placed us. You are no accident and certainly not a mistake.

The repair piece is done by choosing differently. Choosing to live according to God's values and guidance. Choosing to let Him be the God of your life instead of seizing that role yourself. When we choose to live according to who we were created to be, we will find the renewal and revival we desire. We will be heading down the path that leads to restoration.

Changing choices and habits is difficult. It takes time, which is hard in the microwave, instant-gratification world we live in. It takes commitment to better oneself and seek God. This is mostly about changing our heart's focus. It takes the surrender of a person's will and the acceptance of God's path. That is difficult to live in a world that promotes self-exaltation. The good news is that it is not entirely on you to change yourself. In fact, if you try to change on your own, you will fail. God never leaves you or forsakes you (Hebrews 13:5). As you focus on Him, you will find your desires align with His, and that produces change.

All people need restoration. Sin, which is living against the commands and will of God, has broken every person on this planet. Whether you are the victim or the perpetrator (we have all lived both roles), you need a restoration.

My heart is for those who are broken and are looking for hope. Restoration is possible! Repeat that to yourself right now and every day. Believe it! It may take time—years or even decades, depending on the situation. But it is possible for those who work on themselves and who seek out the God who restores.

Now, I must include a crucial point here. This is not what you may want to hear, but it is necessary. Restoration does not always take place as we want it. We are not promised *our* ideas of restoration. Sometimes our ideas are different than God's ideas. OK, most times our ideas of restoration, including the how and when, are different than God's plan. I am saying that life might look different than we might think after restoration takes place. But be assured that His restorative plans are better! He sees all who are involved, not just you, and desires their restoration as well (which takes time). His purposes are good and loving. My prayer is that you will discover the truth of this love as you move through this book.

THE RESTORATION MANUAL

The Bible is full of stories of restoration, more than can fit in this book. In fact, the entire Bible is a story of restoration. In Genesis 1, we are told of God creating the heavens and the earth from nothing. He created all things: sky, land, water, plants, and animals in the sky, land, and sea. Then, in Genesis 1:31, God put the final additions on all His creation by creating man in His own image. "And God saw everything that He had made, and behold, it was very good" (Genesis 1:31 ESV). I remember occasions when I was a young kid who had just finished completing a creation out of Legos and being so proud that I looked at it, smiled, and thought, *Oh yeah! That is awesome* (modern-day version of *very good*). That is the visual I get of God.

Unfortunately, perfection did not last. Two chapters after creation is completed, the man and woman, Adam and Eve, are deceived; and this perfect creation is smeared with sin (earthquake moment). This seed of sin would infect every human being from that point forward. Throughout the entire Bible, God issues covenants to provide a way back to restoration with Himself. But the seed of sin continues to poison man. In the end, Revelation 21:1 (ESV) describes how God restores His creation: "Then I saw a new heaven and a new earth, for the first heaven and the first earth had passed away, and the sea was no more." God eradicated sin from the world and gave us a new creation from which "He will wipe away every tear from their eyes, and death shall be no more, neither shall there be mourning, nor crying, nor pain anymore" (Revelation 21:4 ESV). I eagerly anticipate that day. Restoration completed!

ALL GLORY TO GOD

As mentioned previously, this book contains my story of offense and the pain I caused to many people. In telling these things, I seek to bring glory to my Lord Jesus Christ, who, through the power and work of the Holy Spirit, is healing me from the pain in my past, both old and recent, and is bringing me through a restorative experience both personally and with many whom I love. I seek no personal honor for myself in the telling of my events, for a sinner who shares their experience can only point in awe at the grace and healing found in Christ as they are restored. Restoration on this side of physical death is more of a journey than a destination. The destination is eternity with our Lord when pain and sorrow will be no more (Revelation 21:4). To protect the people involved in my offense, some details will be withheld or vague. However, the details are not as important as the point. It is not the telling of the offense that gives hope and encouragement. It is the story of restoration that comes by way of God that needs to be told. I seek not my glory but His in the telling of His deliverance in my life.

My prayer is that this book may reach the life of a person who has been affected by an earthquake event and finds themselves in the "valley" lacking hope. Maybe that is you, and your desire is for your own restoration story. Maybe you know someone in that valley, and you want to know how to help encourage them. Maybe you caused the earthquake and are struggling with guilt, shame, and the fallout of it all. I pray that your story, whatever it may be, leads you powerfully to know and love the God who is able to restore all things. He has done it many times before, and He is still in the restorative business. You are never too far gone to experience the goodness that God offers. He is a God of grace and loves His creation like nothing else. He adores you!

In the spirit of giving praise to my God, I want to call upon some lyrics of a song (as I will do in all chapters). This song, "Look What You've Done," was written by AJ Pruis, Keith Smilth, Matthew West, and Tasha Layton. It was recorded by Tasha Layton.[3] This song reflects the position I am in now. I can look back and recognize the amazing story of God's grace in my life. God has done and is doing an amazing work; and all the glory, honor, and credit belongs to Him. He is a Restoring God!

> Look what You've done
> Look what You've done in me
> You spoke Your truth into the lies I let my heart believe
> Look at me now
> Look how You made me new
> The enemy did everything that he could do
> Oh but look what You've done.

Earthquakes change lives!

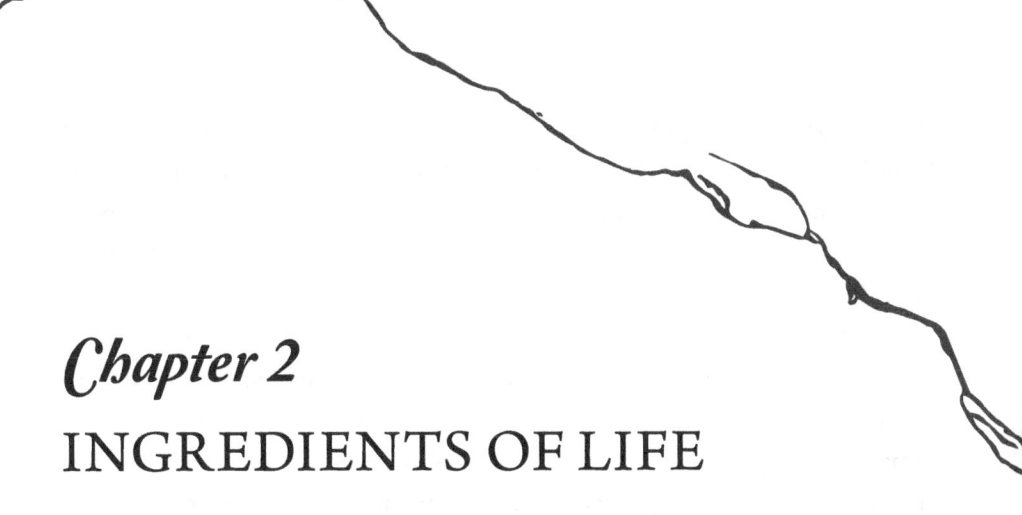

Chapter 2
INGREDIENTS OF LIFE

> I have been crucified with Christ and I no longer live, but Christ lives in me. The life I live in the body, I live by faith in the Son of God, who loved me and gave Himself for me.
>
> —Galatians 2:20

FAITH

Dan was in the hospital, where he was dying from cancer. His one wish was to have a chair by the side of his bed. His wife, Carolyn, asked for their pastor to see him and offer any encouragement to Dan. Mike, their pastor, came and found Dan awake yet resting. He saw the chair and thought that Dan must have known he was coming.

"I see that you have been expecting me," said Mike.

"No, Mike, I did not know you were coming. Why did you think that?" said Dan.

Mike responded, "Well, I saw the chair here and just assumed, I guess."

"Oh, the chair. Yeah, that belongs to Jesus."

Puzzled by Dan's response, Mike asked him to talk more about the chair beside the bed.

Dan told him how he used to struggle with prayer until one day, a friend told him that prayer was just talking to God. He encouraged Dan to pull an empty chair and visualize Jesus sitting there with him. Jesus had promised, "I'll be with you always" (Matthew 28:20), and that empty chair helped him trust in God. He could not see Him, but that empty chair helped strengthen his faith that he was being heard.

Faith is a big deal! Faith is a foundational ingredient in the recipe of a person's life. Outside of love, which is the greatest ingredient (1 Corinthians 13:13) and binds all things together, faith is mentioned most consistently by Jesus toward His followers. It is mentioned over 250 times in the New Testament, revealing how significant it is to a person's life. Jesus was looking for faith in a person's life. He taught that "if you have faith and do not doubt, ... whatever you ask in prayer, you will receive, *if you have faith*" (Matthew 21:21–22, emphasis mine). Often, when He would heal or perform a miracle, Jesus would respond with words such as "Your faith has healed you" (Matthew 9:22) or "Because of your faith" (Matthew 9:29). Other passages would say, "And when Jesus saw their faith" (Mark 2:5). When correcting and teaching His disciples, Jesus would remark about their faith. He would say, "Because of your little faith" (Matthew 17:20) or "O you of little faith" (Matthew 6:30, 14:31).

> *Faith is a critical value to possess.*

Faith is a critical value to possess. So what is faith? How do you get faith? How do you strengthen your faith? Why is faith so important? These are important questions to understand. Since the Bible talks so much about faith, what does it say about it?

What is faith? The best definition of faith comes from the Bible: "Faith is confidence in what we hope for and assurance about what we do not see" (Hebrews 11:1). Faith involves confidence and assurance. Some other translations use words such as *conviction, certainty,* and *evidence toward unseen things.*

Perhaps the most common analogy of faith involves a chair that we would sit down upon. How often do you pull the chair out from the table and, without looking too closely, bend your knees, transferring your full weight onto the chair, trusting that it is going to support you? We do this often. We do not inspect the chair and perform tests to make sure it is suitable for sitting. No, we trust it is there and will support us. That is the confidence and assurance that faith requires. Think about the various things in our lives that we place faith in. There are many examples in our everyday lives. We set alarms, trusting that they will sound off at the correct time for which they are programmed. We buy food at the store with little knowledge of where it has come from but with confidence that it is going to be good for us to eat. We deposit money in the banks and have assurance that we will be able to access it when the need arises. Faith is not a concept that is foreign to us.

How do you get faith? Faith is what manifests when we trust without needing proof. When we trust without needing to use our eyes. Can you see the wind? No, you cannot. You can see and feel the effects of the wind, but you cannot see the wind. So using other senses helps our faith. I am amazed when watching a visually impaired person venture out using their walking stick. There is a measure of faith by which that person is living. Certainly, they use other senses, but they must have confidence that the ground is not going to give way or that the path is clear before them. How do they take that first step? Then the second and so on? It is by faith.

Faith does not come naturally to us. It is so much easier to trust that which we can see. This is why experiences are often such a good teacher. Experience makes trusting easier. Faith is making a conscious choice to trust. It is a choice that says, "I can't see what's ahead or where this is going, but I believe that what I hope for is going to be there." This can be tough and downright scary at times. When the magnitude of the choice's endgame is life altering, faith can be daunting. A stronger faith helps us move forward in our lives.

How do you strengthen your faith? Faith is a muscle that needs to be exercised. Faith starts out with a step and grows with each further step. The first time you put your faith in alarm clocks, grocery stores, and banks, maybe you had a little apprehension that grew into trust. You found that with every use, your confidence improved. This is often how faith grows. Putting your faith in action causes it to grow. Just as an athlete trains their muscles to compete better, so we need to work our faith muscle to live better. This comes easier and more comfortable with experience.

Faith is a foundational part of our lives. Every person puts their faith in something to help operate from day to day. This "something" is the object of our faith, and it helps to ground us. What is the object of a person's faith? People often place faith subconsciously in a variety of things to help stabilize and support them. Some examples include addictions (drugs, alcohol, food); other people; their jobs; and their possessions, among many more. The problem that arises from these is that they are not strong enough to be a person's foundation. Food, alcohol, and drugs are limited and run out. People come and go throughout our lives. Jobs do not serve you; you serve them. Our possessions all fade over time. In Matthew 7:24–27, Jesus compares these to shifting sand that people build their lives on. These foundations may last for a brief time but fail to support lifelong.

There is only one foundation that is strong enough to last and support every person without fail. This is found in a relationship with Jesus Christ, the Son of God. The reason this foundation is strong enough is that it does not rely on us. A person cannot always be strong enough to support themselves. Our spirits can be overconfident in the good times and then quickly become weak and frail when adversity faces us. Jesus is the solid rock foundation mentioned in Matthew 7:24–27. He is our creator. He knows us intimately. The Bible says that the number of hairs on our heads is known (Matthew 10:30). He understands us personally. The Bible says that "because He [Jesus] Himself has suffered when tempted, he is able to help those who are being tempted" (Hebrews 2:18). He has endured every emotion we have endured. He cares for us completely and lovingly. The Bible says that "neither death nor life, nor angels nor rulers, nor things present nor things to come, nor powers, nor height nor depth, nor anything else in all creation, will be able to separate us from the love of God in Christ Jesus our Lord" (Hebrews 8:38–39). Jesus knows us. He understands us. He cares for us. When we accept this and make Him our foundation, we find the object of our faith that can support and sustain us in any storm.

Having a personal relationship with Jesus Christ requires faith. It means abandoning faith in yourself and placing it on "Jesus, the author and perfector of our faith" (Hebrews 12:2). It is the foundational ingredient in the recipe of your life.

INGREDIENTS OF A RECIPE

Who we are comes from a culmination of our experiences. Who we are is much like making a recipe. My mother is a wonderful cook. She makes many wonderful meals and loves to bless other people with them. She makes a great vegetable beef stew, and there are many different vegetables that she prepares to put into the stew. Each one adds a distinct flavor. Then, she would add the beef and let it simmer for hours. It would taste so good.

Our lives are just like this stew. There are several ingredients that go into the making of who we are. I can think of many characteristics of myself that have been shaped by the experiences in my life. Some I will share in the coming pages. This is a foundational concept because as I tell my story, and as you think of your story, it is important to know what has shaped us. It is important to understand how the good and the hard stuff of us was developed. It is helpful to understand what the foundation of your life is built upon. What developed the positive parts of you? What have you allowed to feed and grow the negative stuff about you? Usually, the harmful stuff (negative habits, impure thoughts, and destructive tendencies) is fed by influences we do not even realize we are being affected by.

Many years ago, I was given the challenge to write a description of myself in one sentence. It surely is a more challenging thing to do than it might sound like. What types of things would I include to appropriately describe who I am as a person? What is it that makes up who I am? Certainly, I would want to focus on the good parts of me. But if I am honest with myself, would that tell the whole story of who I am? I ran across this old fragment in a pocket in my Bible from that challenge years ago. That first attempt read, "Brian Goodwin is loved by God but held by hurt."

Even at that early age, I saw two sides of myself. I understood that I was loved by God. That has been foundational to my life. I thank God for the spiritual influences of my parents, friends, and the church I had in my youth. However, the latter half revealed something about me that was also foundational. This was the hidden part of my life. I was "held by hurt." I did not understand it then, and it has taken much of my life to deal with it. It was a key ingredient that shaped my identity.

What was the source of that hurt? Where did it come from? This hurt was like a weed in a garden, choking the good plants to prevent them from growing. Jesus tells a parable in Matthew 13:24–30 where the weeds are sown among the good plants to destroy them. The sower of the weeds was the enemy, Satan. This is exactly what he was doing in my life, and he was using different "weeds" to destroy me. Looking back, I see how he used weeds such as my sensitive nature, my love of music and people, and even my relationship with Jesus as tools to "steal, kill, and destroy" my life (John 10:10). Let me dive a little deeper here.

Sensitive

I am a sensitive person. I am a teddy bear with a big heart. My outward demeanor may look otherwise, but I am a softy. I am that guy that may cry at "feely" commercials. I am a rom-com lover. I am an encourager who loves to show people that I care. In fact, those were the two words (I care) I longed to hear more than any other while growing up. I may often have a stern, serious look on my face, which is more of a learned defense mechanism. Look tough, and no one messes with you, right? However, once people get to know me, my friendly, sensitive, and caring nature is quickly recognized.

Where does this come from? Someone could just say that God made me that way. I would agree with that but not in the kind of way that just blindly believes that from the womb, I have been a sensitive person. Over the course of my life, there have been certain experiences that helped shape my sensitivity—several specific instances in my life where I have suppressed pain. I remember wanting to swim at my seventh birthday party, but after a day of house hunting, the pool was closed when we got back to the hotel. I remember going to a music conference and waiting anxiously for my parents to come and watch my performance, yet they did not show up. I remember listening to friends sound off about their troubles and empathizing with them but never getting a chance to share my own pain. The pain I experienced has developed my sensitivity and caring nature toward others.

Another fact is that I am a middle child. My brother is twenty-three months older (not two years, mind you), and my sister is eighteen months younger (you can just say a year). There is a belief about the middle-child syndrome (MCS), and there are some interesting claims regarding it. According to Sarah Regan, in an article from MindBodyGreen.com, she lists five common traits of middle children.[4] This is a list of some of them:

1. They are peacemakers and pleasers.
2. They are independent and focus on friendships.
3. They try to fit in.
4. They are competitive.
5. They act out to get attention.

MCS is not medically proven, so it is merely a concept. Still, I can relate to most of these traits.

In the family dynamic, I am a younger sibling but also an older sibling. There are dynamics that differ when interacting with older versus younger siblings. *Woman's Day* magazine ran an article titled "20 Things That Only Middle Children Understand."[5] Some of them really hit home for me and have played a role in my sensitivity:

1. Being independent from a young age–The attention wasn't on you, so you had to entertain yourself.
2. Getting awkward introductions–"This is my oldest. This is my youngest. This is the other one."
3. Not having an identity–I was known as Trevor's brother or Shelly's brother.
4. Constantly being compared to your older sibling–The teacher's treatment is based on what they thought of your older sibling.

This led to some challenges since my brother and I are vastly different.
5. Seeking ways to stand out–Your personality was how you made your mark on your family. Yes, personality was my middle name.
6. Living in hand-me-downs–Yes, I got what Trevor outgrew.
7. Always being the peacemaker–I do not like fighting.

My sensitivity, when not guarded, has allowed emotions to drive the train of my life instead of being the by-product of my experiences. When emotions drive the train, it usually ends in a wreck. Emotions should never be the conductor driving a person's life.

Music

Music is a major part of my life. Throughout my school days, I played drums and percussion in all types of bands (jazz, dixie, marching, and concert). I was the first one to bring a drum into my church and have played it during services now for decades. I love to sing as well and have been involved in a variety of choirs and music teams. A valued memory of mine was traveling to Honduras as part of a ministry band. We played rock music and talked about Jesus to whoever came to our concerts. I love to play music.

Music is like medicine to the soul. I love to listen to all forms of music. Sometimes I listen to worship music to simply sit still and hear my Savior speak. I have created a playlist of songs that reflect what my heart and mind have experienced throughout the various stages of the valley I have been walking through. This playlist has been used to encourage and strengthen me. As I tell my story, I will share lyrics that guided and encouraged me through each stage. As I reflect on what has made me who I am, a song titled "Highs and Lows," written by Hillsong Worship and Hillsong Young & Free, describes my faith and my relationship with Jesus,[6]

> Highs and lows
> Lord, You're with me either way it goes.
> Should I rise or should I fall?
> Even so
> Lord, Your mercy is an even flow.
> Should I rise or should I fall?
> You are faithful through it all.
> You're too good to let me go.

What you put into yourself determines what comes out. This is true for any type of influence in your life. If you feed yourself garbage, then garbage is what will come out. If you feed yourself healthy things, healthy things will come out. I had let many unhealthy musical influences speak into my life, and consequently, the output was an unhealthy focus on self. This is detrimental to a life being lived by faith in God. Much of mainstream music glorifies the focus on the self. I can sing along with an uncountable number of songs that promote doing what you want, when you want, and with whom you want. The rhythm and groove may be enjoyable and may seem harmless but, if unguarded, can develop a mental trail that leads to hurt and pain as your focus is kept solely on yourself. Influences are a big ingredient in your life.

People

I am an extrovert. I enjoy being around people and often recharge by being around them. I am convinced that there is not a person out there whom I cannot have an enjoyable conversation with. I welcome the challenge to find something that a new person and I might have in common to talk about. A conversation may start with news, sports, and weather, which is relatively safe. But with time, I can find out, for example, that we both have an uncle named Jim. I love this.

People can be such a valuable source of strength and support. God has wired us for community. The best moments in life usually happen with other people. We are meant to share life together. People celebrate together in the grand times. People cry together in painful times. People help one another when one has fallen. People support when there is brokenness. There is such beauty when this is put into action.

However, pain can arise when people are used, abused, and taken for granted. When helpers feel unappreciated, unrecognized, overlooked, or ignored, the enemy takes something that was good and twists it. I am guilty of this. A significant source of pain in my life has come from letting my good intentions toward others be transformed into pain through *perceived* neglect. Perception, i.e., what I think is reality, can often be mistaken. It is a weed that can distort healthy growth. I am a people pleaser (see above comment on MCS), and too much emphasis has been placed on other people's perceptions of me. More on this in the next chapter.

Jesus-Follower

There is nothing more important in my life than my relationship with Jesus. I have lost my way at times, but when I slow down and refocus, my faith helps lead me back to my values. My heart yearns for all people to experience the amazing grace that Jesus offers freely. I cannot fathom where I would be without this relationship. From my first decision to follow Jesus at the age of twelve to my most recent breath, He has been

1. my refuge in the storm,
2. my rock on which I stand,
3. my Savior from my sin,
4. my light in the darkness,
5. the provider of my needs,
6. the truth I lean on,
7. the way to freedom and hope,
8. my sustainer from day to day,
9. my comforter in the loneliness of life,
10. my peace amid the pain,
11. my joy in every trial, and
12. my *everything*!

So how could this also be a source of pain in my life? The problem lies with one word: *sin*. We all have a sin problem that, when unchecked, causes us to lose faith and rely on ourselves. In effect, the real question is, who is allowed to be the God of your life? Are you going to claim that title? Or will you surrender and allow your Creator, All-Powerful, Sovereign above All Things, Everlasting Savior, Ever-Present Help to be God of your life? This should not be a difficult decision. However, at times, we lose our way. I call this the civil war that rages inside the mind of the follower of Jesus. (Think of the angel speaking on one shoulder and the devil on the other.) One side of me wants my way, the other yearns for God's way. The battle is real. When we choose wrongly, pain and hurt prevail. Faith helps us choose God's way.

JOSEPH

In Genesis 37–50, the story of Joseph's life is told. His story is that of a family that becomes fractured and separated because of sin. It is a story of a family's restoration. Throughout the story, Joseph showed incredible faith and integrity. It shows us that no person's story is lost by God, rendering them unusable. God is in the business of using things that were meant for evil and turning them into stories where people are restored and saved (Genesis 50:20).

Joseph was the most loved son of Jacob. He was given an ornate robe by his dad as a gift. In these two details alone, you find ingredients that would fuel a fire of sibling rivalry among his eleven brothers. In fact, Genesis 37:4 says, "They hated him and could not speak peacefully to him." They were not feeling love for their brother. It sounds like a toxic atmosphere at home. Now, I am not sure what Joseph was thinking, but he has two dreams that he shares with his brothers. The essence of both dreams was about his brothers and parents bowing down to him. You can imagine how this detail is like adding gas to the fire because of his brother's distaste for Joseph.

In Genesis 37:12, Jacob sent Joseph to his brothers, who were out in the field. Joseph went after his brothers, and from a distance, they spotted him. The brothers, who had been plotting for many years now, saw the occasion that was given to them and decided to kill him. They concocted a plan on how to explain the death to Daddy, and they threw him down into a cistern (which was a dried-up well). As they sat down to eat and finalize the story, they saw a caravan coming toward them. A lightbulb appeared over Judah's head, and he saw a chance to profit off his brother. They brought Joseph up out of the pit and sold him to the caravan. As the money jingled in their pockets on the way back to Jacob, they took the ornate robe, ripped it to shreds, and covered it with blood before delivering the disparaging news of Joseph's apparent demise to their dad, Jacob.

Meanwhile, Joseph was taken by the caravan to Egypt and was sold as a slave into Potiphar's house. Potiphar was the captain of the guard for Pharaoh. Genesis 39:2 tells us that "the Lord was with Joseph, and he had success in whatever he did." The master noticed his success, and Joseph became his "numero uno" guy. He was made an overseer of Potiphar's house and over all that he had. Genesis 39:5 says that the Lord's blessing was on all things because of Joseph. It says that Potiphar had no concern about anything but the food he ate because of Joseph. Joseph found a good place after all that had happened to him.

Keep in mind that Joseph was a teenager at this point, and he was "handsome in form and appearance" (Genesis 39:6). This is where Joseph shows some real faith and integrity. Potiphar's wife cast her eyes (Genesis 39:7) on Joseph and tried to seduce him. She said to him, "Lie with me." Joseph's response was amazing. A powerful woman was coming on to him with impure motives, and Joseph's response before leaving was "How … can I do this great wickedness and sin against God?" (Genesis 39:9). That is amazing faith and integrity. The text says this happened several times.

During the final time, she grabbed his garment. In fleeing, Joseph left it behind. Having been refused for the last time, she called to the men of her household and accused Joseph of the dirty deed that *she* had been performing. When Potiphar heard of this, Joseph was thrown into prison. (Side note: I think Potiphar knows the reputation of both Joseph and his wife, and so prison is the punishment. Any other man would have been executed.)

Joseph found himself at the bottom again. It was another setback in his life when he had not done anything but live by faith. Still, the Lord was with Joseph, and he found favor in the sight of the keeper of the prison (Genesis 39:22). Just as before, the Lord made Joseph succeed in all he did.

I can see a lesson here at work. We should always live with faith even when trials come our way. Our faith should make us stand out from the crowd, and this is appealing to the leaders in our lives. Our faith helps us to reflect the goodness of God in our lives, even when trials come upon us.

While in prison, two members of Pharaoh's court found themselves put into custody with Joseph. We do not know what led them there, but there they are. They both had similar dreams one night, and Joseph, the dreamer that he was, interpreted the dreams with God's help. It is good, restorative news for one of them and bad, actually lethal, news for the other. The good news for the cupbearer was that he was restored three days later, as Joseph's interpretation foretold. Joseph hoped this man would remember him after being restored, but that was not the case. It is important to cling to faith during moments when you feel forgotten. I believe Joseph did.

Several years later, Pharaoh had a dream that none of his magicians and wise men could interpret. The cupbearer told Pharaoh about what Joseph had done before. He was quickly summoned, shaved, changed, and appeared before Pharaoh, who told his dream. Joseph, with faith and all, told that only God could interpret dreams. Then, Joseph gave Pharaoh the lowdown about what it all meant: seven years of plenty followed by seven years of famine was the forecast. He followed with a remedy: let Pharaoh appoint a discerning and wise man to set over the land of Egypt to see it through this coming time. It was not a surprise that Pharaoh chose Joseph to be that man. In twenty-five verses, Joseph went from being in the pit of prison to being second only to Pharaoh himself. Talk about a restoration in the middle of a restoration story!

Fast-forward to seven years, Joseph the governor managed the grain magnificently in the plenty years. There was so much grain stored up (does grain have an expiration date?) that the whole country was ready to endure seven years of famine. Genesis 41:56–57 says, "When the famine had spread over all the land, Joseph opened all the storehouses and sold to the Egyptians, for the famine was severe in the land of Egypt. Moreover, all the earth came to Egypt to Joseph to buy grain, because the famine was severe over all the earth." This included Joseph's brothers. They came to buy grain from Egypt, but they did not know that they were buying grain from Joseph.

In Genesis 42, the brothers came to buy grain, but they did not recognize Joseph. However, Joseph recognized them. Joseph wanted to see if they had changed, so he led them on a little rabbit hunt. In the end, he saw that the brothers had been moved to guilt and sorrow for what they had done to Joseph. Moved by their sincerity, Joseph dropped the bomb on them that he is, in fact, their long-lost, sold, rejected, tossed-away-like-last-night's-trash brother. Oh, would not *that* have been a scene to be a fly on the wall for. Imagine jaws hitting the ground like an Olympic weightlifter dropping a bar of weights to the ground. In the end, Joseph's original dream came true as they bowed to him. The brothers then rushed back home to get their father and plan the move to the lush region of Goshen to be near Joe.

The proud scene is found in Genesis 46:29. Joseph had been waiting for the return of his brothers but mostly his father, Jacob. Joseph went up to meet his father, and when he presented himself to him, it says he "wept on his neck a good while." The restoration of this fractured family is one of incredible joy. It shows that God is able to restore any family or person who is fractured because of sin. Have faith!

JOSEPH MIXED WITH MY EXPERIENCE

I am amazed at the faith of Joseph. Joseph was unfairly sold into slavery, but he responded by being the best slave he could be. He was unfairly accused and sentenced to prison, but he responded by being the best inmate he could be. He was unfairly forgotten initially by the cupbearer, but when called upon, he gave God the credit and interpreted the dreams of Pharaoh. When the brothers came to buy grain, Joseph did not respond with hate and anger. His actions led to making God-ordained restoration possible. The ingredients of Joseph's life are filled with hurt and pain, but his faith helped him rise above and let God have the honor in this restoration story.

My past had pain and hurt as well, and I would love to say I responded with the same level of faith as Joseph. That was not always the case. But in and through the pain, God was already at work, preparing me for my own story of restoration. The ingredients of my life have shaped me. I realize that many other people have suffered far greater amounts of pain than I have, and my heart goes out to such. May God get the glory in my story as Joseph gave in his story. He is a restoring God!

PERSONAL QUESTIONS

1. Where is the object of your faith? Is it in yourself or in Jesus to save you from your sin?

2. How would you describe yourself in one sentence?

3. What are the ingredients of your life that have made you who you are?

4. What positive and negative influences do you give license to speak into your life?

5. What do you find fascinating about Joseph's story of restoration?

Faith is a critical value to possess.

Chapter 3
HOLDING ON (TO THE WRONG STUFF)

> Truth Jesus said, "If you hold on to My teaching, you are really My disciples. Then you will know the truth, and the truth will set you free."
>
> —John 8:31–32

TRUTH

It was a quiet Saturday afternoon. The sun was shining outside the office window, and the view of the backyard was peaceful and serene. I was achieving productivity while working on a project that had been pushed back to tomorrow for weeks now. It was a great feeling to finally get the time to work on it. However, I should have had a suspicion that mischief was afoot. Life with three kids under six (at the time) only experienced quiet after bedtime and in the presence of mischief. With my wife out running errands, I thought that letting them watch a movie would distract them long enough to get something accomplished. Suddenly, the quiet was erased with the sound of shattering glass from the kitchen. I was out of my chair and in the kitchen in three agile moves to find the flowers I had given my wife all over the wet floor. Glass was shattered all around them. From five steps away, just outside the arena of mischief, were two sets of stunned eyes the size of hubcaps staring back at me. After instructing them not to move because of the glass, I quickly cleaned up and asked them to sit on the couch. Meanwhile, I thought of how to approach the interrogation.

The obvious first question was "What happened?" All I got were blank stares.

"Can someone tell me how the flowers fell to the ground?" More blank stares.

I asked my oldest if he knew the story and would tell me. He just shook his head and claimed not to know. Amazingly, this was the same for my oldest daughter. Two people were present, but there were no witnesses to the apparent suicidal-vase incident. I just wanted the truth. Neither wanted to admit what happened. Guilt has a funny way of doing that to a perpetrator.

After I discussed the situation with each of them privately, they finally confessed that my oldest wanted to get to the cookies on top of the fridge, but he slipped while standing on the island and hit the flowers. The message given to them is that regardless of the situation, it is always best to tell the truth. Vases can be replaced, and flowers can be put back in water. However, the chance to tell the truth will come and go. Always be up-front and honest—the lesson successfully given.

What is truth? You could take a thousand people from all cultures and walks of life and throw that "meaty" question out there, and you will get hundreds of thoughts and opinions. In writing this chapter, I asked several people and searched various resources to finish this sentence: Truth is _____? The responses were diverse. Here are some statements that I found:

1. Truth is the property of being in accord with fact or reality.[7]
2. Truth is a judgment, proposition, or idea that is accepted as true.[8]
3. Truth is a statement about the way the world actually is.[9]
4. Truth is the aim of belief.[10]
5. Truth is what is right in the world. (Anonymous)

The Human Systems Dynamics Institute differentiates four types of truth.[11] These four types are objective truth, normative truth, subjective truth, and complex truth. Objective truth is what exists and can be proved in this physicality. For example, the sun rises in the east and moves across the sky every day to set in the west. Normative truth is what we, as a group, agree is true. An example is that we have labeled *day* to be that part of each twenty-four-hour period when the sky is lit by the sun. Then, there is subjective truth, which is how the individual sees or experiences the world. For one individual, today might have been a good day, while another person might see today as a tough day. Finally, there is the idea of complex truth, which recognizes the validity of all three truths and allows you to focus on the one that is most useful at any given time. In these cases, we might note that the sun is up, the day is bright, and Mom is in a good mood, so let us take advantage of that.

As I reflected on the above statements, I see a common thread running through them all that truth can change. Can truth change? If reality changes or is different among people, does that mean that truth changes? If what is accepted changes, does truth change? As the world changes, does truth change as well? If beliefs change, does truth change with it? As varied are views of the world, does truth change with each of them? So the base-level question to wrestle with is this: if truth can change, is it really the truth? What are the consequences of truth that can change? Could unstable truth be what leads to disagreements, political infighting, and wars?

The fundamental point of truth is this: Truth does not change. Truth is constant. It is reliable and calculable. We can learn the most about truth by going to a source that has not changed in the many thousands of years since it was written. That source is the Bible. The Bible has plenty to say about truth. Through His words, Jesus claimed to be truth. Jesus's words found in John 14:6 say, "I am the Way, the Truth, and the Life." What does Jesus mean when He says this? How can He be "truth"?

In David Guzik's commentary,[12] he says this about Jesus's statement, "This declaration is a paradox. Jesus' *way* would be the cross; He would be convicted by blatant *liars*; His body would soon lie *lifeless* in a tomb. Because Jesus took that path, He is the way to God; because He did not contest the lies, we can believe He is the truth; because He was willing to die, He becomes the channel of resurrection—the life to us."

Jesus is truth personified. All things were created through Jesus and for Jesus (Colossians 1:16). He is the Creator and, thus, the author of truth. These are facts that do not change.

In addition, Jesus's words in John 17:17 tell us that "the Word is truth." This refers to the Bible. In this historically accurate, proven-through-prophecy, spirit-filled book, we can find the truth to guide us in our lives. We are instructed to walk in truth (3 John 1:3), love the truth, and believe the truth (2 Thessalonians 2:10–12). The benefit of knowing the truth, in Jesus's words, is that it will set you free (John 8:32).

Truth is more than facts. It may involve facts, but it also includes beliefs. It is the way things really are. Truth is more than just a moral guide. It is the very foundation for our lives, just like faith from the previous chapter. Faith and truth are strongest when bound together.

Truth can lift you above any pain. Jesus spoke the truth. In one sentence of truth, He could turn an argument or situation on its head. In John 8, the teachers of the Law approached Jesus with an adulterous woman and tried to trap him.

"What should we do with her?" they asked.

After drawing in the dirt and waiting a little while, Jesus stood and said, "Let any one of you who is without sin be the first to throw a stone at her" (John 8:7). One sentence is issued, and the truth given is that we are all sinful people in need of saving. This is a truth that does not change and that can lift you above your pain.

THE PAIN IN LIFE

Max Lerner says, "The turning point in the process of growing up is when you discover the core of strength within you that survives all hurt."[13] Pain of various kinds is inevitable in life. The question is, how will you respond to it? Perhaps the worst thing that a person can do is suppress their pain and not deal with it. Part of maturing is learning to deal with the pain in life.

Jesus told us that we would have trouble in this world (John 16:33). He does not sugarcoat His messages by telling us that life will be rosy if we follow Him and trust Him as our Savior. There is an enemy that hates Jesus and comes against His followers with lies, deception, and anything that will misdirect us. This is why Jesus gives us a warning about trouble. Life *will* be hard, so be prepared for it.

I was not prepared. From an early age, I chose to follow Jesus. However, my life's foundation was not yet built on the truth of God's Word, and thus, I was not ready to handle the attacks of the enemy. In fact, I did not even realize the attacks were happening. I could not see a simple fact. The pain in my life was a direct result of buying into untruths or lies.

I often bought into lies and deception about who I am and about my self-worth. In fact, my self-worth was based on a false equation. In his book *The Search for Significance,* Robert S. McGee talks about the equation of self-worth that the enemy sells to people.[14] The equation is that our self-worth = performance + others' opinions. We base our value on the success of our performance. Have we achieved at work? Are we thriving in our involvements? We also base our value on how we perceive others think about us. Do people like my look? Do they think I am good at this or that? Do they care about me? This can eat a person up with worry, shame, and fear. There is no truth in this kind of thinking because it constantly changes. It can also push people you are trying to please away. In return, it causes you to try harder and harder to impress them, which pushes you further down the spiral of defeat. It is an endless trap. This was a major problem for me.

The balance between these two components varies for each person. Some struggle more with performance issues, and some struggle more with people pleasing. For example, when I arrive for lunch at school, the seat next to my friend is open. As I move to sit down, my friend says that the seat is already taken by someone else. People confident in themselves would understand that it had nothing to do with them but that the seat was already spoken for. An insecure person who has based their self-worth on other people's opinions would hear that voice in their head saying, *They really do not want you to sit with them. The seat was not really taken.* That person does not see the lie that is being spoken into the battlefield of their mind. They are being deceived.

"If what we think doesn't reflect truth, then what we feel doesn't reflect reality." This is a quote from Neil T. Anderson's book *Victory over the Darkness*.[15] This quote explains what has happened throughout a significant part of my lifetime. I have dwelled on untruths inside my personal thoughts as a way of coping with any negative situation. My thoughts would rationalize what was happening to help me understand, albeit negatively. This could happen in so many circumstances. Some examples:

Circumstance	Initial Thought	Resulting Emotion
Friend declines lunch invitation	I'm not important to him	Sadness
Score low on important work metric	My boss is going to think poorly of me.	Worry, Stress
Wife doesn't show concern for me	She doesn't respect me or care for me	Heartache
I am overlooked for a promotion	I am a loser who will never succeed	Despondence

Negative circumstance to thought to emotion chart

Now, in each of these situations, there is probably a legitimate reason. Perhaps in these examples, the friend had a prior commitment, and the metric didn't take a unique event into the criteria. The wife was overwhelmed with her own tasks, and the promotion needed someone with a different skill set. So in these examples, the truth was not being acknowledged. Therefore, the thinking does not reflect the truth. Thus, the resulting emotion does not reflect reality.

I have experienced such a cycle in my life. In this cycle, it generally started with a circumstance that was perceived negatively. It might be a response taken as a form of rejection. It might be an unsupportive comment or a host of other things. This negative circumstance led to negative thoughts: "I'm not good enough," "I'm unloved," or some other untruth that, in my head, sounded legit to rationalize the circumstance. These negative thoughts then led to negative emotions. These emotions tore me down until I was weak. This is usually where food would enter the picture, and unnecessary eating would take place, a personal vice in my life. The last part of the cycle is where I would realize the impact that the negativity created, and I would suppress it to avoid dealing with it. While this was occurring, I made sure to wear a happy face to avoid being labeled as dramatic. Eventually, I would focus on my faith and pray to regulate myself.

The problem with this cycle is that it does not correctly deal with the pain. The suppressed feelings are still being held on to and not being dealt with. The suppressed emotional pain rots away at the core of who I am. This is not healthy, and it is a common problem. The truth found in Jesus is the necessary healer that helps me to rise above pain.

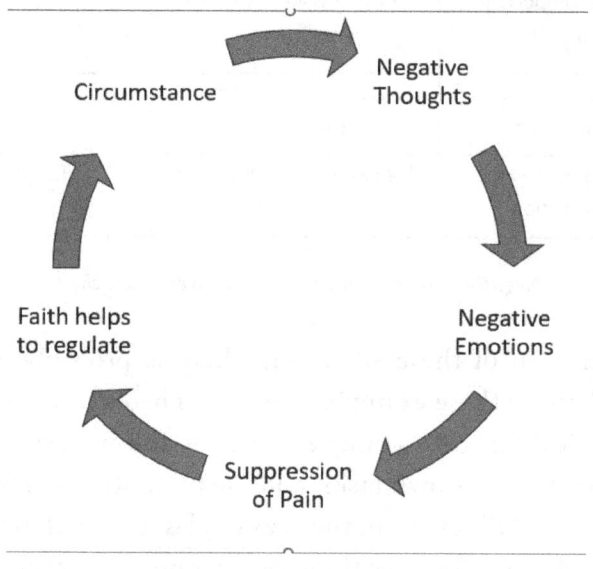

Unhealthy thought and emotion cycle

Spiritual warfare is a very real thing. The enemy speaks lies into our lives to deceive us, to steal our joy, and to destroy us with untruths with the goal of spiritually killing us and our families. Ephesians 6:12 says, "For we do not wrestle against flesh and blood, but against the rulers, against the authorities, against the cosmic powers over this present darkness, against the spiritual forces of evil in the heavenly places." When we find ourselves responding in unhealthy ways, be it within our own self or with another person or group, we must acknowledge that the issue is not with that person at the root level. It is a spiritual battle.

ISRAELITES AND JUDGES

Throughout the history of the Israelites, there were many times when they forsook truth. On many occasions, the Israelites' behavior revealed the futility of people in general. The final verse in the book of Judges illustrates how God's people live when their focus leaves their Lord and God. Judges 21:25 says, "In those days there was no king in Israel. Everyone did what was right in his own eyes." When everyone does what is right in their eyes, the result is eventually destruction, brokenness, chaos, or a mix of all and more.

One of the most common sentences that describe the Israelites is found multiple times in the book of Judges: "And the people of Israel did what was evil in the sight of the LORD" (Judges 2:11, 3:7, 3:12, 4:1, 6:1, 10:6, 13:1). Simply put, the Israelites would forget the truth. They would forget that "I will not leave you or forsake you" (Deuteronomy 31:6). They would forget "And I will walk among you and will be your God, and you shall be my people" (Leviticus 26:12). When we forget the truth, we eventually go through a painful cycle.

In the book of Judges, the Israelites, God's people, went through a constant cycle. The people experienced judgment and the consequence of their disobedience to God. There would be a fallout from their most recent idol worship or other unfaithfulness to God. Often, they would be sold into the hands of their enemies. When it would finally get too much, the Israelites would cry out to their Lord. The Lord would hear their cry and send a judge to save them from their enemies. They would repent of their unfaithfulness and choose the Lord's way. At least until the judge died and went away. Then, the process would be repeated.

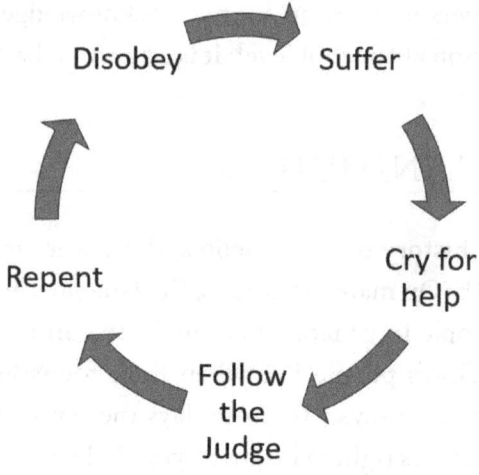

Cycle in the book of Judges

Amid these cycles, the book of Judges contains one story of restoration after another. The list of Judges includes Othniel, Ehud, Deborah, Barak, Abimelech, Gideon, Tola, Jair, Jephthah, Ibzan, Elon, Abdon, and Samson. Judges 3:7–11 is the story of Othniel. It reads,

> The people of Israel did what was evil in the sight of the LORD. They forgot the LORD their God and served the Baals and the Asheroth. Therefore, the anger of the LORD was kindled against Israel, and he sold them into the hand of Cushan-Rishathaim, king of Mesopotamia. And the people of Israel served Cushan-Rishathaim eight years. But when the people of Israel cried out to the LORD, the LORD raised up a deliverer for the people of Israel, who saved them, Othniel the son of Kenaz, Caleb's younger brother. The Spirit of the LORD was upon him, and he judged Israel. He went out to war, and the LORD gave Cushan-Rishathaim king of Mesopotamia into his hand. And his hand prevailed over Cushan-Rishathaim. So, the land had rest for forty years.

Do you see the cycle at play in this short story? The Israelites disobeyed by doing what was evil in the sight of the Lord. (The truth was denied.) As a result, they were sold into the hands of Cushan-Rishathaim. The people cried out to the Lord for help, so the Lord raised up a deliverer, a judge, to save them. The Israelites repented and were saved from their bondage. Then, the people rested until Othniel died, and they again began to disobey.

TRUTH BREAKS THE CYCLE

> *If we set our focus on Jesus and let His truth transform our mind, we will experience the freedom that we desire.*

Many people experience a destructive cycle in their lives that keeps them from living free. The Israelites showed it during the time of the Judges, and I have seen it at work in my life as well. I am confident that you have seen it in your life to some extent as well if you think about it. This cycle continues because we get deceived. When we are deceived, we do not live by the truth. Truth is what breaks the cycle. More specifically, Jesus is what breaks the cycle. If we set our focus on Jesus and let His truth transform our minds, we will experience the freedom that we desire (John 8:36). Deception is a key weapon of the enemy, and humanity has been buying it in bulk since creation. Beware of the battles playing out in your mind. That is the battlefield. Do not suppress your negative thoughts. Expose them verbally; thoughts sound different in your mind than when spoken. Find someone safe you can be vulnerable with and get help. Suppressing negative thoughts and beliefs about yourself is poison. Jesus is the antidote. He is the truth that heals.

Leanna Crawford wrote a song with Matthew West and AJ Pruis entitled "Truth I'm Standing On."[16] These are some of the lyrics that spoke to me during my journey. They gave me encouragement and confidence to stand on the truth of God's Word while traveling the course of the valley.

> This is the truth I'm standing on.
> Even when all my strength is gone.
> You are faithful forever and I know You'll never let me fall.
> Right now, I'm choosing to believe
> Someday soon, I'll look back and see
> All the pain had a purpose
> Your plan was perfect all along.
> This is the truth I'm standing on.

PERSONAL QUESTIONS

1. What do you think about truth?

2. What do you think about spiritual warfare and Satan's attacks on people? Does he attack you?

3. Do you live with a constant destructive cycle? Do you know the truth that will help you break the cycle?

If we set our focus on Jesus and let His truth transform our mind, we will experience the freedom that we desire.

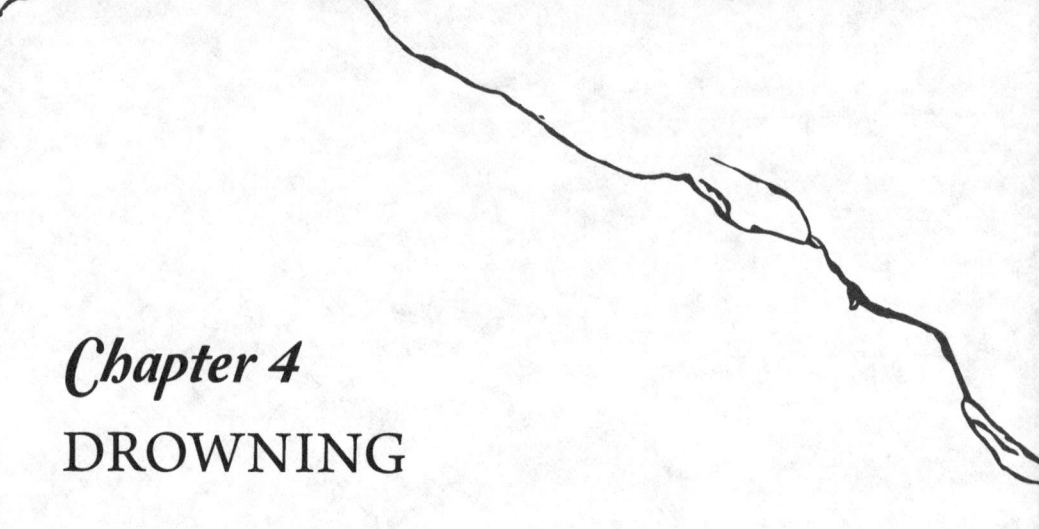

Chapter 4
DROWNING

> Show me Your ways, O Lord, teach me Your paths, guide me in Your truth and teach me. For You are my God my Savior, and my hope is in You all day long.
>
> —Psalm 25:4–5

GUIDANCE

In 2022, I took a baseball trip with my mother. We saw four baseball games in four different cities and visited the filming location for the movie *Field of Dreams* in Dyersville, Iowa, before driving home. It was a memorable trip. Late one night, after leaving Chicago and heading toward St. Louis, I was driving southwest in Illinois along Interstate 55 toward Bloomington. I knew that once I got there, I just needed to turn southeast and drive a "short distance" to get to my destination for that night. I did not think it was necessary to look at the maps. I knew the way. My mother thought there might be a quicker way. So she put her navigator hat on and researched the map. She did some calculations and watched the road for our location. After a few minutes, she spoke up, "You know, if you take this exit coming up, you could take a back road directly to our destination. It would save us about forty minutes."

She was right. It saved us a lot of time because it was a more direct route. The night was getting late, and I was thankful she looked for an alternate route. Life gets easier when we have guidance. Her guidance helped us that night.

Guidance is a needed help in your life. Guidance helps point you in the right direction. Often, the road you naturally want to go on is wider and easier to see down. Guidance may show you the narrow road that takes you where you should go. When you are driving, GPS apps are great at guiding you to where you want to go in a quicker way.

Your life needs guidance. I am sure you can think of a time when GPS helped you navigate a quicker path toward a destination. This is the same for the direction of your life. However, it seems that in life, most people are more apt to set off on a path of their own choosing and go for it without consulting some form of help. That is the sad reality in our lives; guidance is not always sought after or accepted.

Why is guidance often not sought out in our lives? Is our sense of control so heightened that we feel we know what's best? Do we not see the danger that can come with forging the path forward on our own? We are often blind to the pitfalls around us. We can be prone to ignoring our weaknesses and our tendencies that distract our focus just to get what we want. Then, we set a path that may direct us right through those traps. How good would it be to have someone to offer sound advice from an outside perspective? It is even better when we listen to that advice and consider it.

Accepting guidance requires a level of maturity. It is maturity that allows us to accept that we do not always know what is best. Maturity tells us that it is OK to not be a master of everything—that some people may know more than we do—and it is best to be open-minded to what they have to say. Then, we consider their advice to make a more informed decision.

When the idea of writing this book was given to me, I remember chuckling to myself. English was my weakest subject back in school, and I never enjoyed writing papers or essays. Give me a math problem, and I am on it because I love problem-solving. In my mind, I told myself that I was not a book writer. However, the more I thought about it, the more I felt compelled and excited to do it. I had all kinds of ideas about what I would put into the book. But I wondered what the best way was to go about writing a book. I did not know how to start.

I found guidance through three sources. First, I have a friend who had written a book some years ago, so I decided to ask her for advice. She gave me some practical guidance. She said to start with an outline. Gather your thoughts and organize them. Let a few others read your work as you go and listen to their comments with an open mind. These were helpful comments that guided me.

Second, as I moved along and completed sections, having other people read and comment challenged me to be more concise and direct. Talking with others and discussing ideas helped guide my thoughts as well.

Third, I sought guidance from the Holy Spirit, who prompted me with the idea in the first place. He gave me guidance as I started to gather, organize, and outline. He brought me to scriptures that I could use as support. He brought stories of restoration to mind and paired them all up. His guidance was instrumental and pivotal to the whole process. Undoubtedly, without guidance, this book would never have happened.

The Holy Spirit's guidance is seen throughout the entire Bible. In the Old Testament, the spirit would come to a person and guide them to do some incredible things. An example is when you read the story of Samson in the coming pages. In the New Testament and in our current age, the Holy Spirit is a gift given to Jesus's followers as a guide. The Bible promises that those who have repented and chosen to follow Jesus as their Savior from their sin will receive the Holy Spirit (Acts 2:38). This incredible gift resides within the believer (1 Corinthians 6:19). The Holy Spirit is called our helper (John 14:26), our teacher (Luke 12:12), our power (Acts 1:8), and our comforter (Acts 9:31). In Him, we can find the ability and strength to do all things. The Holy Spirit is the power source that rose Jesus from death, and this same power resides in every believer (Romans 8:11). The Holy Spirit is the ultimate guide for a person's life.

LOSING MY WAY

My wife and I had been heavily invested in ministries. On our tenth wedding anniversary, we discussed what we wanted to focus on for the next decade as a family because our kids were growing. We prayed about this and decided to model a life focused on serving others.

At the time, we did not know how we would go about doing that, but we trusted the Lord to provide us with opportunities. Shortly after, I got involved with an international Bible study ministry. This ministry would later require a heavy involvement for both Kara and me as we rose to staff-level positions. I accepted a leadership position within the ministry, which would require me to give thirty-minute lectures each week to over one hundred men. I also had the responsibility of leading each week's training of my group of leaders. It was a heavy time commitment for both of us. I do not regret this at all; however, looking back, I was not prepared for the toll that all the responsibility would take on me.

It was in 2019 when life began taking a sharper downward turn. It had been moving that way in the years prior, but the acceleration grew at this time. The battle in my mind was growing fiercer, and I was getting hit hard with attacks from the enemy that I was unprepared to fight. I was overcommitted to several ministries and activities, which was stretching my time and energy thin. I was running myself into the ground physically and was tearing myself apart mentally. On the outside, nothing appeared to be wrong. I "masked" my issues well in public.

There are natural laws that work against a person. You must work at preventing these deteriorating factors. Say that you take a desk job. Sitting for a great amount of time will cause your leg muscles to get weaker. You must protect this by getting up and moving several times throughout the day. It works the same if you stretch yourself too thin with time commitments. If you overstress yourself and do not take self-care or breaks, you are going to break down. The truth is, if you do not guard yourself against destructive tendencies in your life, you will be susceptible to losing your way.

For married couples, if you do not work at your marriage, it will suffer. Like a plant, it will not grow unless watered and cultivated. Time and connection are two vital ingredients to a healthy marriage. When children come along, you must make time to grow your marriage together, or you will grow apart—no exceptions. Kids require a lot of time and attention. However, you must save some time and energy for your marriage. Your spouse should be your best friend and supporter. If he or she is not, you need to call a time-out and refocus together. Get professional help and guidance if necessary.

As you grow older, you must take better care of your body. If you do not, it will deteriorate, and you will get slower and less sharp. Make the choices to change bad habits and get help and guidance if needed. This can be such a hard thing to do. Habits are so difficult to change.

Lastly, busyness can be a killer that destroys marriages, families, and individuals. There is no shortage of things to get involved in. Work never stops, and there is always more to do. Programs are always looking for volunteers. We can never give enough time to our spouse and kids. We always want more time for our hobbies, activities, and responsibilities. We all have the same amount of time. Create boundaries and live them out to honor a life of balance. Easy to say but hard to do.

My life reflected all this, and I did not see the severity of the damage I was doing. I knew I was running myself ragged, but I did not do anything about it. My wife and I have four teenage kids. As they were growing, there always seemed to be a reason date night needed to be abandoned that week. We did not pray together. We did not take time to work on us. In short, we were growing apart, and this relationally driven person was starving. In addition, I was not taking care of myself and my health. I was not sleeping well, and I was doing nothing to correct it. I was not eating well, and diabetes took hold. I was stretched so thin with my time commitments that I was not in balance. My mental life was suffering from buying into many untruths. It is always easier to believe and rationalize a lie than accept the truth. I suppressed my pain inside. I was pretty good at masking all of it in front of people. I have done that most of my life. The truth is, inside, I was losing my way. I was drowning.

Life can be synonymous with problems. Nobody wants problems in their lives, but they are inevitable. With so many different variables in your daily life (people, work, kids, weather, etc.), you really should anticipate problems daily. In fact, Jesus even warned you about this and gave you encouragement. Jesus tells you that life will have its share of problems, but keep your eyes focused on Him. He is greater than anything that you may experience (John 16:33). You can find incredible hope and comfort in that promise! He has overcome! This is the truth you need when you are lost in life.

Have you ever been lost in life? You find yourself dealing with something that has you confused and looking for help. You are searching for answers but do not really know what the questions are. You are wondering where to go, what direction to take, and who to listen to, among many other questions. It has you stuck, lacking motivation or feeling aimless. If life has not already blown up, you may feel like it is about to. You know you need help and guidance. But how? Who? Where? What?

This was where I was stuck. I was overly busy. I was dealing with painful lies born out of untrue thoughts. I often felt unloved from my perceived rejection or a lack of affirmation (my love language). I was not taking care of myself and felt like I was losing at life. Life was surrounded by negativity. All this was from the enemy who was trying to destroy my family, my marriage, and myself. I believe the enemy did not like all the ministry and serving my family had been doing. I had not noticed the target it put on our backs. The enemy was firing away, and I was not doing anything about it.

SAMSON

There are many interesting and intriguing stories in the Bible, and the story of Samson is right up there among the bizarre. In the last chapter, I wrote about the Israelites during the time of the Judges and mentioned the cycle that was played over and over. Samson was one of the judges of that time. In Judges 13–16, Samson's story is told. Samson took a Nazirite vow, which meant he was committed to the service of God (Numbers 6). Taking this vow meant he was to abstain from alcohol, avoid defilement that came with touching dead things, and let his hair grow. Could you imagine never getting a haircut in your life? Taking this vow meant that you were special and set apart for the service of God.

Samson, however, did not live this way. Samson forgot who he was. Basically, he lost his way. He took a vow that meant he was not to have anything to do with grapes. However, in Judges 14:5, Samson was hanging around a vineyard. Samson was not to have contact with anything dead. However, in Judges 14:9, Samson was eating honey out of a dead lion. Throughout his story, Samson was in deep with his weakness. His eyes were constantly on people (mostly women) and the things around him. When he wanted her, he demanded it (Judges 14:2). When he was angry, watch out. He would yield his incredible gift of strength for selfish purposes. In Judges 15:3, Samson was angry at the Philistines, so he caught three hundred foxes and tied them in pairs by their tails, fastening a torch to them. Then, he lit the torch and sent the foxes into the fields, burning up the shocks, grains, vineyards, and olive groves.

As you read his story, it is stated five times that the "Spirit of the Lord came upon him." The Spirit of the Lord gave Samson incredible strength that allowed him to do incredible feats. In Judges 14:6, Samson tore a lion apart with his bare hands. In Judges 14:19, Samson was tricked by his wife into giving her a secret answer (not the only time this happens); by doing so, he must pay when the men at the feast answered his riddle. To pay up, he went to a nearby city and struck thirty men. In Judges 15:5, Samson was bound while being led to the Philistines. When they came at him, he shredded the ropes; and taking a fresh jawbone of a donkey, he went on to strike down a thousand men. Incredible strength was a gift that the spirit would give Samson, which allowed him to be capable of amazing things that could have been used in service to the Lord as his vow was intended. Samson, however, used this gift for self-serving purposes.

Samson was a leader among the Israelites as a judge. The Philistines, whom the Israelites were subject to, were constantly trying to solve the secret behind his strength. They would eventually find their answer through Samson's biggest kryptonite: women. Samson had a tendency to find women who were wrong for him. His first wife was a Philistine, one of his enemies. In Judges 16, he discovered Delilah. She would be another channel for the pain and ruin to come into Samson's life because he did not guard his heart. A lesson for all people is to know your weaknesses and guard yourselves against them.

Delilah was approached and offered a huge bribe from the Philistines to find out the source of his strength and let them know. She accepted.

Delilah asked not once or twice or even thrice about the secret. She asked Samson four times because he misled her the first three times. Each time, he would wake up with her putting that method to the test and failing. You would think he would get the clue that she was up to no good. Finally, Samson relented and told her the secret of his hair. Just as before, he woke up shaven, and Judges 16:19 tells us that "his strength left him." The next verse clarifies even further by saying "that the Lord had left him." His eyes were promptly gouged out, and he was subdued and taken as a prisoner.

Samson reads as a story of someone who lived for himself. There is no verse saying that Samson had sought after God or served Him as his vow should have led. Samson is a classic case of living life as we want and not seeking guidance. It seems that it wasn't until he had lost everything that he came to the stark reality that he was only who he was because of the Spirit of the Lord coming upon him. When we fail to remember the truth of God in our lives, we will lose our way. We need guidance to help get that back. Samson had an awakening. Life changed. Sometimes it takes hitting rock bottom to shake us up.

> *When we fail to remember the truth of God in our lives, we will lose our way.*

Judges 16:22 carries incredible hope for those who have been broken. Samson lost his way, and it finally caught up with him. It says, "But the hair on his head began to grow again after it had been shaved." We are never too far gone. God is able to restore what is lost. God never forsook Samson, even when he was disobedient. God's mercies were there for Samson even in a Philistine prison. All Samson had to do was turn his heart back toward God and receive them.[16]

The only mention of Samson calling to the Lord is found at this point. In Judges 16:28, it says, "Then Samson prayed to the LORD, 'Sovereign LORD, remember me. Please, God, strengthen me just once more, and let me with one blow get revenge on the Philistines for my two eyes.'" Samson had been paraded around as entertainment at a sacrificial gathering to their god. Samson asked to be placed between two pillars that supported the roof that held about three thousand people. Samson prayed and asked for God to avenge him by strengthening him one more time. It was a suicidal act that would leave Samson dead. As the story finishes, Samson experienced a restoration of strength, and the pillars were pushed away.

We could say that Samson was restored with self-renunciation. This last great victory only came when he was broken, humiliated, and blind. He could no longer look at himself. Samson's life shows the danger of underestimating our own sinfulness. He probably figured he had things under control with his own fleshly lusts, but his selfish desires led directly to his destruction. Rather than break his relationship with Delilah, he allowed it to break him. Samson was the great conqueror who never allowed God to properly conquer him.[17] My advice (and Samson's, I presume) is to let God conquer you. Seek Him for guidance.

GUIDANCE HELPS PREVENT LOSING YOUR WAY

One of the most dangerous things we can do in our lives is to go at it alone. We were not created to be loners. We were created for the community. Samson's life shows the danger of being a loner as a leader. It seems that everything Samson did, he did alone. I also have been a loner at times, even though I classify myself as a people person. I enjoy being with people, but too often, I am merely superficial and fear going deep. A person needs friends to help them. Family can also be an aid. Without them, we can be prone to losing our way.

Wisdom is seeking guidance from trusted sources. Mentors are especially important. A mentor is an experienced and trusted adviser. They are someone you trust to give guidance when asked or needed. They are not afraid to tell you hard things. These people are as precious as gold in life.

Guidance helps us to see more clearly. From this side of the valley now, I can look back and see more clearly. Perhaps Samson, even without eyes, was able to see more clearly in the end. If you are lost in life or feeling like the attacks of the enemy are coming heavy, take these things into consideration:

1. Are you finding guidance in the Bible daily?
2. Are you spending time in prayer and stillness before the Lord, seeking guidance from the Holy Spirit, daily?
3. Are you living your values?

If you answer no to any of these, construct a plan of action right now to fix it. Call a life audible and get back on track. Seek the guidance of a trusted source. If you do not, there could be severe consequences. It did for me, and it did for Samson.

There is a song that came out in 2017 entitled "Keep Your Eyes on Me" and performed by Tim McGraw and Faith Hill.[18] The title is the line that gets repeated constantly and is such a truth for any person who may lose their way. Keep your eyes on Jesus. Worship Him. Trust Him. Have faith in Him. In Him, you will find guidance to find your way:

> Keep your eyes on me, Keep your eyes on me
> When it hurts too much to see, Keep your eyes on me.
> Keep your eyes on me
> When the light in your heart is too burned out to see
> Keep your eyes on me.

PERSONAL QUESTIONS

1. When have you found the need for guidance in your life?

2. How do you respond to stress in life, and what helps you regulate it?

3. What signs warn you that you may be losing your way, and how do you change course if they show up?

4. Who is a trusted source that you can turn to for guidance?

5. How does the story of Samson challenge you to use your strengths for the glory of God versus the glory of you?

When we fail to remember the truth of God in our lives, we will lose our way.

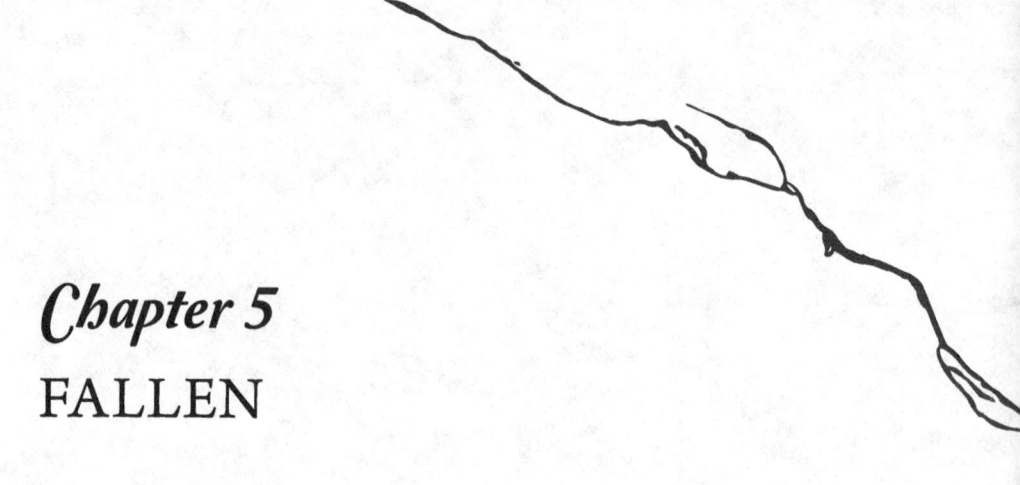

Chapter 5
FALLEN

> If we claim to be without sin, we deceive ourselves and the truth is not in us. If we confess our sins, He is faithful and just and will forgive us our sins and purify us from all unrighteousness.
>
> —1 John 1:8–9

SIN

My wife and I were on the way to the grocery store with kids in tow. It was going to be a quick stop, as shopping with multiple kids often needs to be. As my wife and I were discussing, out from the recesses of the back of the minivan came an odor of immense unpleasantness. It was quickly decipherable that the diapered child had filled his pants with an undesirable mess. We arrived at our destination, and Mom hopped out of the car with her stocked diaper bag ready for the job. She was always prepared. The trunk was opened, the mat was laid down, the kid was nestled, the shorts were off, the diaper was unlatched, and oh! What held before my wife's eyes was synonymous with the worst filth you could imagine. It was brown, soupy, chunky, and powerful enough to make all of us choke on our lunch. Call in the reinforcements. This was a doozy!

The picture I just described, which just about every parent can sympathize with, is how I hope you view sin in your life. Sin is disgusting.

It is repulsive. It is dirty. It is messy. It is painful to clean up. It is hideous. It stinks. I am sure you get the idea. Sin is wretched.

Yet we love our sin. We may not like to admit that and deny it when confronted about it. However, we seemingly enjoy and keep coming back to the things that we know are destructive to our lives. We think, subconsciously, that our sinful desires are going to fill us up and satisfy us. We think this so much that it may become an addiction. Do you know a person who abuses alcohol yet denies having a problem using it responsibly? They continuously run to it to cope with problems. Perhaps a person uses illegal drugs because of the "feels" they get and continues to use even though they know it is destroying them inside. A person hides their use of pornography because it is like candy for their eyes, even though they know it is warping the way they view and treat women.

Sin, in its most basic description, is disobedience to God's commands. In Matthew 22:36–29, Jesus tells us the two greatest commandments to live by are to love the Lord with all our hearts, souls, and minds and to love our neighbors as ourselves. When you think about sin, it always violates one of the two of these. Let us say that you have an elevated focus on money, and you are seeking it with everything you have. This has now become your god, which violates His first command. Perhaps you are lusting after another person, which destroys healthy love toward others and yourself. This violates the second commandment to love others as yourself. So many of our struggles in life come from a violation of these commandments.

Everyone has a vice. Everyone has a sinful struggle, where they wrestle with self-control. The more people I meet, the more I am convinced this is true. It may be an addiction to alcohol, drugs, or pornography. Vices can be other things as well. It might be food abuse, lust, perfectionism, dishonesty, greed, pride, jealousy, or a host of other things. Vices are the things that we run to instead of God when we are struggling with control. This vice reminds us that we need God in our lives.

I love food. However, I can struggle with gluttony. I will find myself eating unnecessarily for no reason. I will eat to cope with stress. I will eat to distract myself from what I should be doing. I will eat with the subconscious thought that it is somehow going to make me emotionally satisfied. Instead, it is never enough. In the end, I usually feel horrible. I am a diabetic now, and this is due to the lack of control over my vice. For me, lack of control over food is a sin. I turn to it for satisfaction and comfort instead of my Lord. Not always, but more often than should happen.

SIN LEADS TO TRAGEDY

I have spent the first three chapters recounting the pain that I have experienced throughout my life, which shaped who I was. This was important to set up this chapter. This chapter is hard for me to write. Before I go further, I want to make an important comment. In fact, this comment is so important to me that I pray it could be a warning for you and others. I am not alone regarding past hurts. We *all* have experienced pain in some form, and most of us are still holding on to it. You are responsible for getting help with the pain you hold on to before it destroys you. Not seeking out help will lead you to sin, and your sin leads you to spiritual death (Romans 6:23). You cannot wait for someone to fix you. You must take that first step toward getting help.

Looking back, I did not know what problem was occurring, but I knew there *was* a problem. I often thought I was the problem. I did not understand why I felt so negatively about myself. I rationalized negative thoughts toward myself. This was a problem, and I did not get help as I should have. In my marriage, I felt so inferior to my wife compared to work, kids, and commitments that I felt isolated and alone. This was a problem, and I did not address it with her in a healthy way. I suppressed my feelings of inadequacy. At work, I did not seem to be having success in what I was doing. I reasoned that I was not any good at what I did and believed that I was a failure. This kind of thinking is a problem, and I did not seek help with it.

This is spiritual warfare. Some people may call it mental illness. I see it as the same. The enemy, Satan, is like a prowling lion seeking someone to devour (1 Peter 5:8). He desires to destroy us, and the battlefield is in our minds. Romans 8:6 says, "The mind governed by the flesh is death, but the mind governed by the Spirit is life and peace." The "flesh" is our sinful nature. What you set your mind toward will determine its health. My mind, with all the negativity, was disobeying the first commandment because I was not seeking God with all my heart, soul, and mind and allowing the Holy Spirit to fix the issues in my head completely. I was disobeying the second commandment because my love for others was weak because of my struggle with loving myself in an unhealthy way. I was letting the enemy win by not owning my pain and seeking help.

Hurt people hurt people. In September 2020, this truth became a reality in my life. I committed a crime against someone. There is no excuse for it, and I am not proud of it. For the protection of the people involved in it, I will not give any more details. For the respect of all involved, I would ask you, the reader, to let any curiosity go. This is not the purpose of the book. The purpose of the book is to remind you that there is a God who is able to restore what a human has broken.

> *Failure is an event, not a person.*

Failure is an event, not a person. This is a quote by Zig Ziglar that I have held on to as truth. This is a quote that became important for me when I was torn down by my shame and guilt. This understanding is at the crux for a person wrestling with how to respond to a person who has committed a sin. Can they separate the person from their failure? Or do they see the person as a failure? It is an identity question. There have been many people who were disgusted with me and saw me as a failure. They walked away from me and spoke out against me. There were those who just did not talk to me anymore. There were also those who stood with me. They saw my failure but did not consider me a failure. They did not condone my actions by any means but were able to separate the two. I had to learn to see my identity not as a failure but as a person who committed a failure. The separation of sin and identity is a major issue for people to wrestle with.

Many of Paul's letters in the Bible start with "To the saints in." This verbiage is important because Paul wanted his audience to understand their identity. He did not want them to identify as sinners, though his letter would challenge the sin that they had been committing. He wanted them to see themselves as saints who have sinned and can stop sinning. Their sin was an event, not their identity.

Jesus is the king of the one-liner. In one sentence, He could say it all, make a point, and end the discussion. An example is in John 8:1–11. The Pharisees brought a woman who had been caught in adultery to Jesus to try and test Him. "The law says to stone her. What do you say?" they asked. I love Jesus's response. He played in the dirt. He made them wait. I envision this driving them wild. The text does not say. Eventually, when He was asked again, Jesus got up and ended the discussion with one line: "Let him who is without sin among you be the first to throw a stone at her" (John 8:7). This would be a mic-drop moment. One by one, they all left. Jesus stood up and asked where everyone went. "Hasn't anyone condemned you?" asked Jesus. Jesus was able to separate the sin from the sinner.

Romans 8:1 gives hope to the sinner who places their faith in Jesus. "Therefore, there is now no condemnation for those who are in Christ Jesus." The term *in Christ Jesus* simply refers to the one who has placed faith and trust in Jesus. If you have done so, then there is no condemnation by God for your sin. He is not sitting in heaven with a lightning bolt ready to strike you down because of what you have done. This does not mean you are given a license to continue sinning. In the preceding story, Jesus told the woman in the end to "go and sin no more." We are to be changed people because of Jesus, and receiving Him as your Savior will start that change. Many times, it is not until we hit the bottom that we realize the change we need in our lives. September 2020 was that cliff for me, and I am deeply sorry to all who were affected by my sin.

DAVID AND URIAH'S WIFE

David is one of the most-known names in the Bible. He was called a "man after God's own heart" (Acts 13:22). He was anointed as Israel's second king and lived as God's chosen. He wrote most of the psalms and was quite a musician as well. If there is a character to name your child after, this would be one of the best. Perhaps the most amazing thing about

David is that he is also known for an egregious sin in his life. Second Samuel 11 tells us the story:

> In the spring of the year, the time when kings go out to battle, David sent Joab, and his servants with him, and all Israel ... late one afternoon, when David arose from his couch and was walking on the roof of the king's house, that he saw from the roof a woman bathing; and the woman was very beautiful. And David sent and inquired about the woman. And one said, "Is not this Bathsheba, the daughter of Eliam, the wife of Uriah the Hittite? So David sent messengers and took her, and she came to him, and he lay with her. And the woman conceived, and she sent and told David, "I am pregnant."

It was springtime, and this was the time of the year when kings went out to battle. But for some reason, David did not go this year. Was he hurt and recovering? Was he sick? We do not know. We only know that David did not go. When we do not do things that we should, that is when we often do things we should not. David went up to the roof and was admiring the view when he spotted something. Actually, a someone. He spotted a woman (Bathsheba) bathing. After this, he *really* admired the view. He liked what he saw and even sent for her. She came to him, and they "got to know each other" quite a bit better, so much so that she became pregnant.

We are prone to using our privileges to gain what we want. David misused the privilege of power as king to get what he wanted. He saw someone (Bathsheba) he wanted and took her. Where there is a will, there is a way. You and I can do this as well. It may not be another person's spouse, but when we desire something with selfish motives, it can consume our desires. This is a problem with the use of credit cards or loans. When we see that thing that we want, and we can buy it using credit, we often do. This is where discipline is helpful. When we give in to our temptations, we often ignore or dismiss the conviction of our conscience. The consuming thought is that we want it.

I often feel this way with pizza. I see it, and it looks so good. So I will get it. However, I am not strong enough just to eat two to three pieces. It is usually like four or five, and that is when I regret it. I feel sluggish because the amount of carbs and sugar I consumed does not mix well with my diabetic situation. A lesson I have learned is that just because I can does not mean I should. Do you know what I mean? David did not recognize the danger of taking Bathsheba as he did. He just took her for himself, and the result was a pregnant married woman. This is adultery.

Nobody wants their sin to become public knowledge. When we have failed, we do not want people to know, especially not anyone in charge who can discipline us, like a parent, a teacher, law enforcement, and even God. I have heard of stories in the news where people have bribed or paid people off so that the truth would not come out. In many TV murder mysteries, this is the reason the murder takes place. Someone is trying to cover something up. The next step for David was to try to cover it up.

David sent for Bathsheba's husband Uriah and called him back from the battle. The thought is that if he could get Uriah to sleep with his wife, it would explain her pregnancy, and David would be off the hook. Well, Uriah did come home, but he would not go home to his wife. He reasoned this was not fair to the men who were out fighting away from their families. He slept with the servants instead and waited to be sent back to the battle. David heard about this and decided that maybe a little alcohol was needed to soften Uriah's convictions. He got Uriah drunk and sent him home to be with Bathsheba, but again, he did not go home. Uriah had the integrity that many of us (including David) need to have when desires rule our thoughts. Seeing that Uriah did not go home again, David sent him back to the battle with a note instructing that he be put on the front lines and killed. To add salt to the wound, after Bathsheba mourned his death, David married her. Do you think Bathsheba ever learned that her new husband was responsible for her first husband's death? David is stuck hard in the middle of his sin.

God loves His followers and takes steps to allow us to turn back to Him after turning away from what we covet. We may have the Holy Spirit rise within us to convict us of our wrongdoing. It may be a supportive friend who sees our faults and is courageous enough to confront us in love to warn us. God may intervene and allow circumstances to delay our dive into sin just long enough for us to become wise with our actions and repent. Will you be discerning to see the grace of God in your life? God sent a prophet, Nathan, to warn David of the sin he committed. Using a story, Nathan was able to snap David out of his completely selfish actions and see the bigger picture of his sin.

There are consequences to every action—good and bad. Nathan informed David that the baby resulting from his sin would die. It is horrible when another person must bear the price for another person's sin. I think of a person who is killed because of a drunk driver. A baby is aborted because the pregnancy is not convenient for the mother. A person suffers abuse because of another person's selfish behavior.

David was crushed by the news of his unborn child's impending death. He turned wholeheartedly to God, pleading for the child. He would not eat. He slept on the floor. I could only imagine David weeping continuously because of conviction over what he did. I too have endured similar intense emotions. It breaks my heart to think of how my sin has affected many people.

The death of Bathsheba's child because of David's sin was a major blow and difficult for them to swallow. Praise God that He does not leave us at the bottom. In fact, in several places in the scripture, God promises never to leave us or forsake us. David and Uriah's wife went on to have another child, and this child would be the next ruler of Israel. Solomon was born to David and Bathsheba, and he would become an amazing king. Regarded as the wisest man to live and perhaps the wealthiest of all time, Solomon started out as a wonderful king for Israel before sin also got the best of him.

LETTING SIN RULE

"If you do what is right, will you not be accepted? But if you do not do what is right, sin is crouching at your door; it desires to have you, but you must rule over it" (Genesis 4:7). These are the words God gave to Cain because of the jealousy he was experiencing toward his brother. Cain did not take this warning seriously, and he killed his brother out of jealousy. There is a lesson for us here. The reality is that we are not strong enough to resist sin. We need the Holy Spirit's help. We need a Savior.

I did not take responsibility for my pain and get help. I ignored the warnings in my life, and it led to a tragedy and a life-altering situation that affected more people than I realized. I did not see the sin crouching at my door, and I let it consume me.

David let sin rule his desires instead of ruling over them. The results were pain and death. A marriage was violated, and an innocent man was killed because of one man's desire. A baby died because of that man's sin. The result of sin really *is* death (Romans 6:23).

Maybe this is you, and you are somewhere along a path of sin that is leading to death. You are choosing to believe that your path will be different, but that is just ignorance. Heed the warnings that the Bible gives over and over. Sin is impactful. Sin is a path that leads to death. You must repent and turn in the direction of God. Maybe you don't know what to do. You know something is wrong, but you do not know how to fix it. Get help. Cry out to God first and ask for His guidance. Seek professional help from a pastor or a counselor who will encourage you to seek Jesus. Do not stay silent, as that is exactly what the enemy wants you to do. Get help.

"Sinner" should not be your identity. Jesus came to rectify that situation. He knew that our sins would eternally keep us from God. So He allowed Himself to be punished in our place to pay the required penalty for our sins. Because of His resurrection, Jesus has defeated death. He wants you to know that if you receive His gift of grace for your sin, you can be forgiven.

David Crowder performed a song that he cowrote with Ed Cash. It is titled "Forgiven."[19] When you understand the grace of forgiveness that is offered to you because of Jesus, it should humble you deeply. His forgiveness issues us the freedom to be restored.

I've done things I wish I hadn't done
I've seen things I wish I hadn't seen
Just the thought of Your amazing grace
And I cry, "Jesus, forgive me!"
Forgiven, forgiven
Child there is freedom from all of it
Say goodbye to every sin
You are forgiven.

PERSONAL QUESTIONS

1. What is your vice? What do you do to guard yourself against your vice?

2. Do you struggle with separating a person's sin from who they are?

3. Have you ever felt condemned for something you have done? How does Romans 8:1 comfort you?

4. Is there a sinful situation you find yourself in and need to repent from?

Failure is an event, not a person.

Chapter 6
DOUBLE LIVING

> Let us draw near to God with a sincere heart in full assurance of faith, having our hearts sprinkled to cleanse us from a guilty conscience and having our bodies washed with pure water.
>
> —Hebrews 10:22

GUILT AND SHAME

Leeches are often thought of as disgusting, bloodsucking creatures. They are feared, and many a scary story involves these little guys. John Flinn, a guide who has taken several groups of people to the Himalayas, tells stories of finding them in people's shoes, on their backside after using the restroom, and often on their legs. However, he tells one story about them that will add to your negative leech perceptions. While visiting the middle hills of the Himalayas with a group of people, he awoke to a woman who was shrieking with a half-muddled shrill. She was screaming, "Ah rot a reech in rah rowf!" Apparently, while she was sleeping, one had crawled into her mouth and affixed itself on her tongue. She could not get rid of it for fifteen minutes while it finished its midnight snack.[20]

You may not have a bloodsucking story that involves leeches, but you may have experienced life-sucking trauma that comes with guilt and shame. Living with these is double trouble for your life and can wreak havoc if not corrected in a healthy way. Let us look at each of them more closely.

Guilt is an emotion one has when they feel responsible for a misdeed. It may be a real or an imaginary wrong. It is an emotion that is often experienced when you feel that you have hurt someone. Guilt can arise from different situations. A child may feel guilty for eating the last brownie when he knew that his sister had wanted it. An employee may feel guilty for missing a mandatory morning meeting after oversleeping. Some guilt can be irrational. A person struggling with perfectionism may deal with irrational guilt. You have expectations for yourself that are higher than the norm, and you experience guilt when you do not meet them.

Guilt can be debilitating. Some of the physical symptoms that may arise from guilt involve poor sleep, digestion issues, increased heart rate, rapid breathing, or dryness in the throat. It can affect every person differently. I was talking about guilt with a friend who had eaten himself to obesity. He connected his weight issues to the guilt he carried from past insecurities. He would eat to comfort himself during his struggles. Another person had a different encounter with food. She lost nearly fifty pounds because of guilt in her life. She had left her spouse for another man. That relationship ended quickly, and she was left alone. The guilt she felt inside because of what she had done would cause her stomach to quake, and she would lose her appetite. She eventually became malnourished because she was not eating. It ravaged her body because she did not deal with her guilt. You could say that her guilt was eating her up. A third person, whom I knew from a counseling group, spoke about how his guilt would cause him to start breathing fast. It would appear like he was having a panic attack. The bottom line is that guilt can be very strenuous to a person's health.

Guilt is something a person must work to understand, deal with, and ultimately let go of to overcome. This can be a difficult thing to do. You cannot change the past, so you must alter the course of your future. You may want to apologize to the person

> *Guilt is something a person must work to understand, deal with, and ultimately let go of to overcome.*

who was hurt, but in some cases, you may be unable to do that. You may want to fix what was broken, but you may be limited in your ability to do that. There are plenty of situations that are out of our control. This is where the circle of influence comes in.

Stephen Covey has a tool called the circle of influence.[21] The circle of influence is a diagram that helps identify what a person should focus on. In the following diagram, there are two circles, one inside of another. Imagine all the things inside the inner circle being all the things that you can control or influence. This may be what you will eat, wear, or do today. It could be how you will respond to another person or situation. It could be how you move forward with a task or job assignment. You are in the driver's seat regarding these things. Next, all the things between the two circles are things that you cannot control or have little influence on. He calls this the circle of concern. It could be as simple as the weather or traffic delays. It might be frustrations such as a friend's angry words or power outages. There are numerous things that we do not have control of. When your efforts are focused on the circle of concern, you will lose time and energy that could be spent on things you can control or influence. It is much more productive to focus your resources on those in the circle of influence. As you do so, your circle will increase in size because you can control more things.

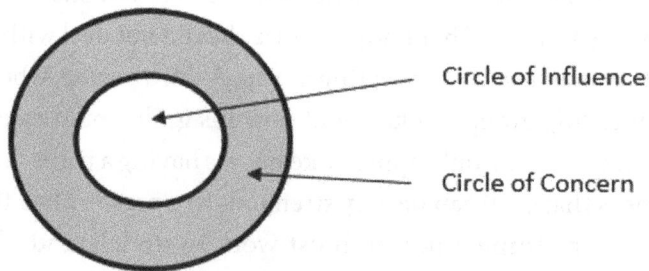

Circle of influence, circle of concern

Much of your guilt lies in the circle of concern. You are limited in your control over the ripple effect of your actions. Focusing on what you can control will help you move forward and deal with guilt. It is important to accept your situation and seek to understand the damage it has caused. You must learn from your past mistakes and seek to become a better person. Visualizing the future in a positive way can also move you forward to a healthier point. Thinking about what you would do differently if put into a similar spot again will help lessen and overcome guilt.[22]

A major hurdle for some people is in taking personal responsibility for what was done. Until you can do this, it will be extremely hard to overcome guilt. You need to find the humility to go to that person(s) affected by what you did and apologize. This falls in line with the circle of influence. You can influence the situation by seeking forgiveness. Now, forgiveness is a process that people need to go through. Often, it takes time to move through this process. However, whether forgiveness is granted at that time or not, it does not matter. You have taken a crucial step, and this will help ease a guilty conscience.

The focus of guilt is on the *act* that caused pain and hardship. Shame is a different kind of "animal." It is more personal. The focus of shame is on the *person* who caused pain and hardship. That is often you. In short, you view yourself as the problem.

Shame is a feeling of embarrassment or humiliation. It comes from your perception, real or not, that you have done something dishonorable, immoral, or improper.[23] Shame becomes problematic when it becomes internalized. Shame is an emotion that makes you feel like a bad person. It can be connected to negative self-evaluation, distrust, powerlessness, worthlessness, or feelings of defeat (not measuring up to your expectations for yourself). When you deal with shame, it generally leads you to an overly harsh evaluation of yourself. A common thought pattern when you are dealing with shame starts with "I am." A person shaming themselves because they failed a test says, "I am so unintelligent." A person shaming themselves because they were left by a boyfriend or girlfriend is "I am no good." The center of shame is oneself.

Shame can be accompanied by a wide variety of symptoms. When you deal with shame, you may have feelings of wanting to disappear. Being around other people reminds you of your offense, and you just want to be elsewhere. Another symptom of shame is anger. When you are feeling shameful about something, and you are confronted with it, it is common to not know how to handle the confrontation, and so anger boils over. You already understand that it was wrong, but you do not know how to respond. Anger can be a red flag that you are dealing with shame. People with shame want to be free from the condemning feelings associated with their shame, and so it is common for an addiction of some kind to take root. Addictions become a coping mechanism for shame but ultimately drive unhealthy habits into your life. People turn to almost anything to help.

Another symptom that shame may be prevalent in your life is feeling overly sensitive or worried about what others think of you. This, in turn, may lead to feelings of being underappreciated, rejected, inadequate, or some other kind of distorted thought about reality. This is a dangerous cycle to be in because there is no end to the depths of our mental depravity.

A problem that usually accompanies shame is denying or hiding your wrongdoings. When you are immersed in shame, it is common to avoid taking personal responsibility for your actions. You may be apt to turn to blaming someone else or using some type of excuse. Be real with yourself. Do you find yourself saying in your head "But they did this" or "Why should I do this when they are doing that?" You are liable to yourself. You control how you respond. Admit when you are wrong and then do better. It is not shameful to admit your wrongs. Swallow your pride and take steps to be a better person. That is respectable.

Shame can be so devastating to a person's life. How can you overcome it? How can you be healed from the accusatory throws of shame?

Overcoming shame starts with being forgiven. God has forgiven you. You can receive His forgiveness by accepting that His Son, Jesus, died an excruciating death *for you* and your sins so that you can be free from condemnation. Reread that last sentence, seek to understand it, then forgive yourself. Forgive yourself! Stop, listen, and observe how you talk to yourself; then have compassion. Practice mindfulness through prayer and come before God in humility. You are so much more than you give yourself credit for. We are our own worst critics. Lastly, recognize when shameful thoughts are present and seek support from trusted people. You are not alone. Try telling yourself that and dare to believe it.[24]

Shame and guilt are common troubles that you will face in your life.

You may think that what you have done or that you yourself are a problem. This kind of shame and guilt are nouns. However, shame and guilt can also be verbs. In other words, these are actions that we can do to other people. This needs to be guarded against. If we are not careful, we can guilt another person into doing something. "If you don't do this, you will feel bad." This is an example of guilting someone into something. "If you don't do this, you are a bad person." This is an example of shaming someone into something. There may be proper uses for these statements, but you must check your motivation.

Guilt and shame can lead you to become a healthier person. You must choose to allow it to grow you. Choose humility, lose your pride, and allow God to refine you out of your guilt and shame.

LIVING WITH A SECRET

I know shame and guilt. I have been living with these double life suckers for a good portion of my life. The interesting thing is that I could not give it a name. I did not understand what was happening inside my thoughts. This darkness I was living in was very real to me, but I learned how to live in it. I did not realize the damage it was doing inside of me.

I lived with the knowledge of something I had done that was shaming me, and it consumed me. I was a follower of Jesus, a Christian. I was supposed to have it all together, right? Morally perfect as I reflected Jesus to others in my life. I was a business professional at work. I was supposed to be in control and in charge. My shaming and guilt-filled thoughts left me feeling anything but in control. I did my best to mask it. However, inside, I was ravaged and wrecked. I was living a leech-infested life. I was living a double life: one life of feeling shame and guilt and one life of trying to appear like I should, whatever that is.

I had been working on finishing my basement for a few years. This is a huge job to do, and I will empathize with anyone who has finished such a project. I had completed all the framing for a bedroom and closet, bathroom, utility room, closet, and a large living space. I had wired all the entertainment ports because I knew how to do that. However, I was stuck with electrical, HVAC, and plumbing needs to be done; and I lacked the knowledge and funding to do that. That added quite a bit of frustration. I finally was able to pay to have someone do that for me, but then came the need to Sheetrock. This is something you cannot easily do on your own. I was getting frustrated at the amount of time it was taking to get things accomplished. I had five people living in the house with me, but no help was offered. It was requested, but any help given was brought with complaining. There was a common emotion that grew during this time: anger.

Anger became my release of pent-up frustration and shaming thoughts. It did not take much to make me boil over. There was one occasion when it all blew up. My wife, kids, and I planned a Sunday afternoon after church when we were all going to get together to apply Sheetrock. I mean, a family who sheet rocks together stays together, right? I have a leadership gift and generally get involved in some kind of leadership in everything I do. I have been wired with the understanding of how to manage, delegate, and maximize efficiency. I had done this for twenty years. Yet here I was, standing in the basement with five people looking at me, and I began barking commands to each of them like a drill sergeant giving orders. Almost at once, I was met with resistance, and it made me blow up. The bomb had been ticking leading up to it, so it did not take much to detonate. The result was more shameful thoughts and guilt.

I was living life with a secret. The knowledge of an offense I had committed, the frustration of a basement slowly progressing, a marriage that was growing apart, and unfulfillment at work were building shame and guilt within me. I participated in a ministry where I was teaching God's Word every week, but each lesson added to my feelings of being a failure. I was supposed to be living like a model believer, but I was failing in many ways. Enter shame-filled thoughts. I was the problem. I should not be teaching this class. There are more qualified people. Why am I doing this job when I am not any good at this? Why doesn't my wife fulfill my every need? I must not be respectable or loved by her anymore. Why can't this basement get done quicker? I am not smart enough and do not know what I am doing. Why did I do what I did? I am helpless. Can you hear all the shaming going on in my head? It was a spiral of despair.

What was my real problem? Was my problem personal pride? Yes! Was the problem shame? Big-time! Was the problem guilt? Definitely! My pride made me think I was good enough to handle all my issues even though my shame was telling me that I was the problem. My guilt just weighed me down and killed my motivation. The real problem was that I was not seeking help. My shameful thoughts told me not to be dramatic and that I did not need help. The reality was that I needed help pointing out that I was so self-absorbed that I could not see what was really going on. I could not see the forest for the trees.

God created people to worship Him. We are to serve one another and to love one another. I was living my life and, subconsciously, believing people should "worship" me, serve me, and love me. I was the boss at work. I was the husband and the father. Wasn't that what I deserved? The answer is no, but I lived as if I thought it was yes. My actions were turning people away. I did not understand why and would reason with shameful and distorted thoughts. I stuffed it and masked it. I would suppress my guilt and shame and use my faith to overcome moments of struggle. However, I was not dealing with the issue. I did not take responsibility for my thoughts, actions, and behavior as I should have. I was a frog in the pot that was heating up, and I was not reacting. I was denying what was out there because of my offense. But it would eventually catch up to me.

PETER AND HIS DENIALS OF JESUS

If there is a characteristic of Peter that I can relate to, it is his impulsiveness. It surfaces several times. In Matthew 14, the disciples were rowing the boat on the rough waters when they saw Jesus walking on the water. Jesus told them not to be afraid. Peter called out to Jesus, "Lord, if it's you, tell me to come to you on the water." Another time, Jesus was telling the disciples that he would die and be raised on the third day. Peter took Jesus aside and said, "Never, Lord! This shall never happen to you!" (Matthew 16:21–23). A third time was when the soldiers and Pharisees came to arrest Jesus in the garden. John 18:10 says, "Then Simon Peter, who had a sword, drew it and struck the high priest's servant, cutting off his right ear."

Simon Peter had a history of impulsive behavior, and he was a leader among the disciples. Like all people, Peter had his moments of failure. There are a few stories that are told in all four gospels, but Peter's biggest failure is one of them. The setup to the failure was when Jesus told His disciples what to expect on the night of His detainment. Matthew 26:31–35 reads,

> Then Jesus told them, "This very night you will all fall away on account of me, for it is written: 'I will strike the shepherd, and the sheep of the flock will be scattered.' But after I have risen, I will go ahead of you into Galilee." Peter replied, "Even if all fall away on account of you, I never will." "Truly I tell you," Jesus answered, "this very night, before the rooster crows, you will disown me three times." But Peter declared, "Even if I have to die with you, I will never disown you." And all the other disciples said the same.

Jesus's response to Peter was personal and detailed. He told Peter that very night, he would personally disown Jesus three times. Peter declared that he would never fall away from Jesus. In Mark, he is quoted as saying, "I will never disown you." In the gospel of Luke, Peter says, "Lord, I am ready to go with you to prison and to death." Peter made it clear that he would not back down. No doubt, a little impulsivity led to this comment. As the story progressed, the soldiers came to arrest Jesus, and all the disciples were scattered as was prophesied.

Peter did not go far, though. In fact, John 18:15 says that Peter and another disciple were following Jesus. Because the other disciple knew the high priest, they were able to enter the courtyard. It was here that a servant girl asked if Peter was also one of the disciples. Peter's response was no. The rooster got up and cocked its head. "C'mon, Peter, you are not going to deny Him to a little servant girl, are you? No threat there." A little while later, Peter was standing by the fire, warming himself around a bunch of people. They asked him if he was one of the disciples. "I am not" was his answer (John 18:25). The rooster cleared its throat. "Ahem." Finally, a servant of the high priest, who was a relative of the guy whom Peter had impulsively cut the ear off, challenged him about being there in the garden with Jesus. Peter denied it. Luke's gospel quotes Peter, "Man, I don't know what you're talking about!" The rooster bellowed. This moment was captured powerfully in the gospel of Luke. Luke 22:61–62 reads,

> The Lord turned and looked straight at Peter. Then Peter remembered the word the Lord had spoken to him: "Before the rooster crows today, you will disown me three times." And he went outside and wept bitterly.

Why would Peter weep bitterly? One word: guilt. He felt such a weight for saying three times exactly what he said he would not. This was a heavy guilt. I would not be surprised if Peter replayed Jesus's look over and over in his head. That look said it all to Peter.

Just like Peter, our guilt can be released. I love that this was not the end of the story for Peter. Jesus was crucified, buried, and then raised back to life. He was seen by hundreds of people. Then Jesus appeared to Peter and others by the lake. He had breakfast cooking for them as he called them in from fishing. Jesus had a personal message for Peter. John 21:15–19 says,

> When they had finished eating, Jesus said to Simon Peter, "Simon son of John, do you love me more than these?" "Yes, Lord," he said, "you know that I love you." Jesus said, "Feed my lambs." Again Jesus said, "Simon son of John, do you love me?" He answered, "Yes, Lord, you know that I love you." Jesus said, "Take care of my sheep." The third time he said to him, "Simon son of John, do you love me?" Peter was hurt because Jesus asked him the third time, "Do you love me?" He said, "Lord, you know

all things; you know that I love you." Jesus said, "Feed my sheep. Very truly I tell you, when you were younger you dressed yourself and went where you wanted; but when you are old you will stretch out your hands, and someone else will dress you and lead you where you do not want to go." Jesus said this to indicate the kind of death by which Peter would glorify God. Then he said to him, "Follow me!"

This was Peter's restoring message. I imagine Peter's guilt eating him up in the three days that Jesus was in the grave. Even after the resurrection, there was an elephant in the room between Peter and Jesus. Jesus believed in Peter and had plans for him to be a leader in the early church. Three times, Peter had to answer to Jesus, just as three times Peter denied Him. But three times, Jesus infused Peter with belief by telling him to feed His lambs, take care of the sheep, and feed the sheep. He concluded by looking Peter in the eye and reoffering the request He made in the very beginning. He said to Peter, "Follow me!" In this story, you can imagine Peter's confidence restored and guilt lifted.

There is a side story of shame that went parallel to the night of Jesus's arrest and trial. Judas Iscariot agreed to betray Jesus by turning Him over to the chief priests and elders. Matthew 27:3–4 says, "When Judas, who had betrayed him, saw that Jesus was condemned, he was seized with remorse and returned the thirty pieces of silver to the chief priests and the elders. 'I have sinned,' he said, 'for I have betrayed innocent blood.' … [Then] Judas threw the money into the temple and left. Then he went away and hanged himself." Judas was filled with shame for his actions. His shame led to his death.

BREAKING FREE

There is hope for those who want to be healed from guilt and shame. You do not need to let these life-sucking elements drain you and put you under bondage. You can experience freedom. The Lord and Savior, Jesus, came to make that possible for you. Jesus freed Peter from the guilt that he experienced after denying him three times. Maybe you have denied Jesus more than three times with your actions and your words. That does not disqualify you from experiencing a restoration of hope that there is more to life.

My guilt and shame put me in bondage from which I would eventually be freed. However, for a season, I was in deep with my guilt and shame. I lost my way and searched. I was not paying attention to the red flags. I was not taking responsibility to seek help. I was living in the circle of concern and focused on those that I had no control or influence over. I had not forgiven myself and did not realize I needed to. As a result, I was sliding further into my shame, and it was making me angry. It was my coping mechanism. My hope was that my offense would never become known, and it would just go away. All the while, the bomb was ticking and about to detonate.

Learning to deal with guilt and shame plays an important part in your restoration story. Tenth Avenue North sings a song titled "You Are More." It was written by Jason Ingram and Mike Donehey.[25] This song encourages me to look at how shame and guilt have played out in my life. My shame and guilt have come from sin. However, God did not create a sinner. He created me to be more.

> Don't you know who you are, what's been done for you?
> Don't you know who you are?
> You are more than the choices that you've made,
> You are more than the sum of your past mistakes,
> You are more than the problems you create; you've been remade.

PERSONAL QUESTIONS

1. What "leeches" are sucking life from you right now?

2. What has caused guilt in your life in the past or present? How did you handle it? How did it affect you?

3. What has caused shame in your life in the past or present? How did you manage it? How did it affect you?

4. Have you forgiven yourself for past sins and offenses against God?

Guilt is something a person must work to understand, deal with, and ultimately let go of to overcome.

Chapter 7
WELCOME TO THE VALLEY

> For if by the trespass of one man, death reigned through that one man, how much more will those who receive God's abundant provision of grace and of the gift of righteousness reign in life through the one man, Jesus Christ.
>
> —Romans 5:17

PROVISION

Guinness World Records are amazing! People have done some pretty incredible feats. Budimir Sobat, a fifty-six-year-old Croatian free diver, held his breath in March 2021 for 24 minutes and 37 seconds.[26a] That is longer than some game shows. Angus Barbieri wanted to lose some weight; and so, in 1971, with the help and guidance of doctors, he went on a fast. He ended up going 382 days without eating. He went from weighing 456 pounds to 180.[26b] He took a few vitamin supplements along the way, but that is a long time between pizzas. There is a record for going without sleep that Guinness no longer recognizes because it could be extremely dangerous to attempt (as if the other records are not dangerous?). However, Randy Gardner, under close observation, went 264 hours and 24 minutes (eleven days) between snoozes.[26c]

Breathing, eating, and sleeping fall under the category of physiological needs, according to Maslow's hierarchy of needs.[27] The reason we know these are physiological needs is that life would end if they were not available. Sobat's breath had to be restored at some point. Barbieri went a long time without eating, but he had a lot of nutrients stored up as weight to help sustain him. That storage would have eventually been used up, and his body would wither. The study done on Randy showed a deterioration of cognitive skills as the days passed. Going without sleep is detrimental to your health and will cause issues. Gardner claimed to suffer from insomnia even some years later. These three guys willingly went without these needs for a time.

The other needs that Maslow describes are safety needs, such as health, security, and employment. There are love and belonging needs, such as friendship and family. There are esteem needs, like respect, recognition, and status. Lastly, there are self-actualization needs, which involve the desire to become the most that one can be. An important part of growing up and becoming more independent is learning how to provide for these needs.

God provides for our needs more than we recognize. He is a God of provision. There may be viruses that we encounter that our immune system, created by God, helps us to ward off. Maybe we are not sure how to handle something on our taxes one year, and He ordains a conversation with a friend in which we discover the solution. There may be a monetary need that we did not foresee, which an unexpected check in the mail would help cover. We could all use more unexpected checks.

God is a need provider. Too often, though, it is easy to lose sight of this fact. You may find yourself suffering from anxiety and worry because you do not know how your needs will be met. Why do people worry and get anxious? Jesus addresses this in Matthew 6:25–34:

> Look at the birds of the air; they do not sow or reap or store away in barns, and yet your heavenly Father feeds them. Are you not much more valuable than they? Can any one of you by worrying add a single hour to your life? And why do you worry about clothes? See how the flowers of the field grow. They do not labor or spin ... If that is how God clothes the grass of the field ... will

> he not much more clothe you? So do not worry, saying, "What shall we eat?" or "What shall we drink?" or "What shall we wear?" For the pagans run after all these things, and your heavenly Father knows that you need them. But seek first his kingdom and his righteousness, and all these things will be given to you as well. Therefore do not worry about tomorrow, for tomorrow will worry about itself. Each day has enough trouble of its own.

God is aware of your needs and takes joy in providing for you. Jesus reminds you in this passage that if God takes care of the birds and the flowers, then how much more important are you, His creation, who is made in His own likeness? He can provide if you trust Him. You must look to Him for provision in every needy situation.

There are times we choose not to receive God's provision. Stress, distractions, or just the gravity of the circumstances we find ourselves in leads to ignorance, whether intentional or not. We ignore the advice given to us. We choose to satisfy a want instead of taking care of a need with our finances. We choose pleasure over responsibility with the use of our time. Our eyes can be so focused on what we want that we miss the provision of a need that God is giving to us. There was a time when I was preparing for one of my weekly lessons. I was dealing with the added pressure that my supervisor was going to be in attendance. I wanted to look extra good during my lecture. I studied and prepared more than ever until I was stressed and stretched thin. I used my sleep time to study and prepare more, and the result was that I wore myself down and got sick. The night of the lecture, we had a big snowstorm, and we had to cancel the night's activities. God provided me the time to rest and recover—and to realize the flaws in my way! It is easy for us to get in the way of God providing for us.

Sometimes God provides for us in ways that we do not see coming. In 2016, my family moved into a house we fell in love with the moment we first viewed it. Little did we know that the man living next door would become one of my closest friends. I had been lacking a close friend for a while, and he was a rock star to me. Also, he had daughters who were close in age to my daughters. Another time, my car was having engine trouble, and I was not having luck with roadside assistance. A man pulled behind me and asked what the problem was. I mentioned the engine, and he asked if he could look. He spent less than five minutes under the hood, and he had it back up and going. It turned out that something had come loose. Surprise provisions can be the best!

> *What if the problems in our lives might actually be what is necessary to give us freedom that we not only desire but also need.*

Now, what if something happens that causes a crisis? It is possible that a crisis is God's provision in disguise. We do not want trouble in our lives. We like comfort. What if the problems in our lives might actually be what is necessary to give us freedom that we not only desire but also need? Laura Story wrote a song called "Blessings." There is a line in the song that says, "What if trials of this life, are Your mercies in disguise." Trials are not fun. However, they can be used by God for provision.

Job is a character from the Old Testament in the Bible who said something remarkable. Job had just been told that his building had collapsed, and he had lost all his children. Also, all his animals and property were either stolen or burned in the fire. He had lost his whole wealth. Job was grief-stricken, yet he looked at the situation and exclaimed, "The LORD gave, and the LORD has taken away; may the name of the LORD be praised" (Job 1:21). Job knew trials. Yet Job did not let trials convince him that God would not provide for him. God uses our trials as a provision to change us to be more Christlike.

ENTERING THE WILDERNESS

I can still remember the day. It was Tuesday, July 13, 2021. I was working for a bottling company and was building a display while talking with my wife. She told me that the local law enforcement had contacted her and that I was requested for an interview. That comment perplexed me, and

I immediately began trying to figure out why. Nine months had passed since I had committed the offense, and I had suppressed it deep down. I had selfishly tried to erase the memory and figured it had gone long enough that it would be taken to the grave with me. The interview was set up for two days later on a Thursday. It became a constant thought, and worry began to set in as I started recalling details from my memory. That night, my wife asked what was going on, and I told her what I suspected it was about. This was the first time she had heard about it and was struck with complete shock.

The day of the interview came, and it was a beautiful, sunny summer day. It would have been more appropriate to be rainy and cloudy. As I look back, the sunshine was a provision by God. The interview began with a series of questions, and I quickly realized what it was about. I tried to show that I was being cooperative. When it ended, I was told to leave and wait for a call before going home or anywhere. I felt my world start spinning, and all kinds of thoughts began swirling. Was I going to be arrested? Was I going to jail that day? What was happening? My thoughts started going down all kinds of rabbit trails. I felt so isolated and alone.

I drove to a local park and sat at a picnic table. I sobbed for an hour or more. I am glad I had my sunglasses on. I was praying and pleading with God. There was a group of teenagers about fifty feet away, and one of them eventually walked over and asked if he could sit with me. He said it looked like I was struggling and asked if I needed anything. He was another provision of God. I declined and just shared that my world had just been rocked, and I had things to process and work through. He asked if he could pray for me, and I, of course, accepted. It was a short prayer, and then he wished me the best. I can remember him saying, "It'll get better." Eventually, the call came, and I went home.

My wife came home that evening; and we talked, prayed, and mostly cried together. Where do we go from here? An earthquake has just happened in our home, and where do we start picking up the pieces? There were questions to ask and temporary answers to be put into place. A key concern was my family's safety. Unfortunately, this meant that I needed to leave. Where would I go? I knew I needed to talk to my parents. They had a basement that was not being used except for my father's office. It had a bedroom and a bathroom. I am sure I could stay there for the short time I would need to be away. That meant I needed to tell them about the situation.

The next day, Saturday, I rode my motorcycle and asked my dad if he wanted to go for a ride and talk. He joyfully accepted. We rode for a half hour before finding a park to sit down. I unloaded the whole story and cried until my eyes hurt. We prayed together and discussed the future. He was shocked and disappointed. Previously, I had been called the golden child by my brother because I could do no wrong. Both of my siblings had challenging times in their past, and I was the one who was "clean." Not anymore. We rode back to the house and told my mother that I would be moving in the next day. Their basement was another provision by God.

My wife and I have played on our church's music worship team for most of our marriage. We were on the schedule to play that next day on Sunday. The music was so personal that day, and both of us remember crying while playing. If anyone was looking at us, they might have been amazed at the passion put into our playing. However, both our spirits were troubled. It is amazing that we were even able to play. I chalk that up to God's provision of enabling. One of the songs, "God of Revival," has lyrics that say,[28]

> There's no prison wall You can't break through.
> No mountain You can't move. All things are possible.
> The darkest night, You can light it up, God of revival.
> Let hope arise, death is overcome, You've already won, God of revival.

This song took on a special meaning in my life. It felt like there was a thick wall in front of us. A huge mountain had risen before us, and it was intimidating. I would shout out the words, "All things are possible," knowing that God could help with our situation. It seemed like darkness had set in, but as I worshipped, God was spreading light. In between our two services, my wife and I found prayer partners, who prayed with us while we wept. We spent the entire thirty minutes with these prayer warriors.

That afternoon, I packed up everything I needed and moved to my parents' basement. In my mind, I was thinking it might be for four to six months. I was very naive about what lay before me. There were two main thoughts moving through my head. The first was Psalm 23:4, which says,

"Even though I walk through the darkest valley, I will fear no evil, for you are with me; your rod and your staff, they comfort me." I felt like I was stepping into a dark valley, and I did not know what the road ahead looked like. It was scary. My second thought was of the Israelites after the Exodus. They did not know it at the time, but they would be wandering the wilderness for the next forty years. I was entering my wilderness.

What is the wilderness? The wilderness is a place for intense personal experience. The wilderness is a training ground. It is a place of relying on God's provision. John the Baptist received the Word of God in the wilderness (Luke 3:2). It is where a person spends time getting life corrected and perspective adjusted. Moses had encounters with God in the wilderness, like the burning bush or Mount Sinai experiences. Elijah spent time in solitude and isolation in the wilderness (1 Kings 19). In that space, he sought the Lord in his troubles. The wilderness is a place where your needs are not met, and you must rely on the Lord. This is where the Israelites were taken after the Red Sea encounter (Exodus 15). The wilderness is a place of renewal. It is a place of testing. Jesus was led to the wilderness by the Spirit to be tempted by the devil (Matthew 4:1).

I did not like that the truth about my offense came out, but it was ultimately what needed to happen. God was providing what was needed for healing. A long road was ahead, but it was a road that would take me where I needed to go. Even through the trials, God has a gracious provision.

ISRAELITES AND THE EXODUS

Joseph invited his father and brothers to live in the land of Egypt during the famine. This was a restoration of a family I detailed in chapter 1. The Israelites then lived in Egypt for 430 years. Eventually, the number of Israelites grew more numerous than the Egyptians. Thus, the Egyptians made slaves of the Israelites to maintain control. Exodus 1:14 says, "They [Egyptian slave masters] made their lives bitter with harsh labor in brick and mortar and with all kinds of work in the fields; in all their harsh labor the Egyptians worked them ruthlessly." They cried out to the Lord for deliverance. Exodus 2:24–25 says, "God heard their groaning, and he remembered his covenant with Abraham, with Isaac and with Jacob. So, God looked on the Israelites and was concerned about them." God had a plan of provision and rescue.

During this time, God raised up Moses, a Hebrew from among Pharaoh's court who had fled Egypt several years prior. Moses, given direction by the Lord through a burning bush, returned to Egypt to confront Pharaoh as a mouthpiece for God. He commanded Pharaoh to let the Israelites go free. If he did not, God would send a plague. Pharaoh refused, and so God sent a plague to come upon the Egyptians. Eventually, Pharaoh relented to break the plague. Once the plague ended, his heart would harden, and they would be back to square one. This cycle went on nine times until the final plague. The final plague involved the death of every firstborn son in Egypt. This was the final straw, which finally broke Pharaoh's hardened heart to let the Israelites go from Egypt.

The Israelites quickly left Egypt and headed toward the Red Sea. Realizing the impact of letting them go, Pharaoh "changed his mind" (Exodus 14:5) and pursued after them. After catching up to them at the Red Sea, God parted the waters to let the Israelites cross on dry ground. This was one miraculous provision! Once the approximately one million Israelites had made it through, the Lord released the waters, drowning the Egyptians in pursuit. The Israelites were free from Egypt at last!

You would think that with such a mighty provision of rescue, the Israelites would be infused with so much faith and trust that nothing could cause them to doubt God. Even while they were leaving Egypt, God was visibly with them in a pillar of cloud by day and a pillar of fire at night (Exodus 13:21). Yet only three days after leaving the Red Sea, here were the Israelites complaining to Moses. "What are we to drink?" they grumbled (Exodus 15:24). So the Lord provided drinkable water. Then, after setting out again, they grumbled again. They remembered all the food they had back in Egypt and complained that they had been led out to die in the desert (Exodus 16:3). Again, the Lord provided. He set up a process where a bread-like product called manna rained down each morning for them. This process would last the entire forty years they wandered the wilderness.

The Israelites continually grumbled against the Lord. They would remember what they had when they were in bondage in Egypt. Then, they would complain about unmet needs. At least, not being met the way they wanted them to be met. We are often prone to doing the same. We see what we want to focus on, and that usually means missing what God is doing. God is a provider, but it is in His way, not ours. We need to tune our minds to be more open to seeing what God is doing than focusing on what we think should happen. His ways are always better. His provision is better.

As the Israelites moved on, they came to Mount Sinai, where they camped, while Moses went up to the top of the mountain for forty days and forty nights. It was here that he received the tablets containing the Ten Commandments. The people grew restless and decided to take matters into their own hands. They had Aaron, the high priest, fashion a calf made from gold that they had all pooled together. Then, they presented their burnt and fellowship offerings before the calf. This made the Lord's anger burn against them and desire to destroy them.

Parents can relate to the Lord's burning anger because of the Israelites' disobedience. We provide for the needs of our children the best we can. We feed them. We provide them with a home and safety. We love them in so many ways. Then, when they disobey, we are prone to getting angry and disciplining them. This is to show them the errors of their ways and to guide them to make better decisions next time. Thankfully, Moses was convening with the Lord on the mountain and interceded for them, or history might have been vastly different. Thankfully, on this side of Jesus's life, He is convening with God and is interceding for each of us who call Him Lord. He is our Savior. He is making a provision for us before God. Thanks be to God for sparing us despite our sins.

In Numbers 13, the Israelites again made a major blunder. They were nearing the Promised Land, and the Lord commanded Moses to send men as spies to explore the land. They must return with a report of what they found. What was the soil like for growing? What were the people like? What were the cities like? Do they call it football or soccer? Twelve men, one from each tribe, were selected for the mission. At the end of forty days of exploring, they returned. Ten of the men gave bad reports with warnings that we are like "grasshoppers" (Numbers 13:33) compared to the inhabitants of the land. The other two spies knew of the Lord's promise and had confidence that He would provide a victory. Moses took all their information to the assembly of Israelites. As Joshua and Caleb, the two spies who trusted the Lord, spoke confidence in the Lord, the whole assembly talked about stoning them (Numbers 14:10). The assembly's faith was not in God's provision.

There was a consequence for the Israelites' distrust. In Numbers 14:23, the Lord told Moses that "not one of them will ever see the land I promised on oath to their ancestors." Their sentence would be wandering for forty years in the wilderness. Eventually, every person who was at the Red Sea miracle would die. But that would not be the end of the story. We have a restoring God, who is patient. The land that was originally promised to Abraham and his descendants would be restored in time. The promise would be fulfilled through the next generation of Israelites. That is the God who provides for us. He is faithful to His promise.

GOD'S PROVISION WAS A WILDERNESS

God's ways can be mysterious, but there is provision through it. Sometimes the provision comes in trials. Sometimes we must wander through the wilderness to get to where He wants us. Many times, what we really need is not what we would expect.

The Israelites had to wander because they refused to trust God to deliver them to the Promised Land. He had provided countless instances before that. When the road ahead was uncertain, was He going to stop then? I found myself in a "wilderness" as I entered what I viewed as "the valley." I did not know what lay ahead, and my prediction ended up being considerably mistaken. The one thing I would come to know is that there was a lot I did not know. "The unknown" would become what I knew. But I also knew that "though I walk through the darkest valley, I will fear no evil, for You are with me; Your rod and staff, they comfort me" (Psalm 23:4). I could trust my God to provide for me.

Ginny Owens wrote a song with Kyle Matthews entitled "If You Want

Me To."²⁹ This song encouraged me during my time in the valley, and it became a prayer for me:

> The pathway is broken and the signs are unclear
> And I don't know the reason why you brought me here
> But just because you love me, the way that you do
> I'm gonna walk through the valley if you want me to

PERSONAL QUESTIONS

1. How have you seen God provide for your needs?

2. How might you be fighting against something that God is providing for you?

3. What discomfort might you be enduring that could be a provision for your life?

4. Have you experienced a wilderness time in life? How did it shape you?

What if the problems in our lives might actually be what is necessary to give us freedom that we not only desire but also need.

Chapter 8
THE FALLOUT

> No discipline seems pleasant at the time, but painful. Later on, however, it produces a harvest of righteousness and peace for those who have been trained by it.
> —Hebrews 12:11

DISCIPLINE

Tara Lipinski is an Olympic figure skater who won gold in the 1998 Olympics in Japan. She was the first woman to complete a triple-loop, triple-loop combination in the competition. At the time, she was the youngest single skater to become an Olympic champion. She was fifteen years old. Tara's competitors were established veterans like Michelle Kwan of the United States, Irina Slutskaya from Russia, and Surya Bonaly of France, who completed a backflip during her competition. Tara's odds were not high to win. Prior to the competition, Tara lacked the Olympic experience of the others. She was much younger than the others, and the pressure was more than she had ever experienced.

In an interview with Molly Fletcher, Tara was asked what it takes to make an Olympic champion. Tara, of course, emphasized the hard work it took. But then, she also emphasized that it was the discipline that helped her tap into her full potential and reach the heights of her sport. She had to train her mind in how to battle. She had to master how to think positively and productively to overcome negative mental struggles. She said she did not feel as talented as the others, so her mental game had to give her the advantage. It takes sacrifice and immense discipline to be elite. Her interviewer chimed in, acknowledging that "people overestimate talent, and underestimate discipline."[30]

Discipline is a word that has positive and negative connotations. Hearing the word *discipline* may invoke memories of the focus and determination it took to reach a goal. It may also reflect the memories of being sent to your room by your parents for being disrespectful. *Discipline* is a noun and a verb. It is something you have (or do not have), and it is also something you do. It took discipline for Tara to make her 4:00 a.m. skating sessions when training (noun). She disciplined herself to stick to her training plan (verb).

Discipline is a set of rules or regulations that are implemented to help achieve a goal. Discipline is training by using restraint in developing self-control. Discipline helps you to be honest, motivated, and hardworking and encourages you to be your best. A mother sending her son to his room uses restraint (the boundaries of his room) to help develop self-control over his use of words by giving him time to think about what he said. An athlete follows a set of rules for himself in training to develop the strength and endurance needed to excel in the sport. Discipline helps us become who we want to be.

There are several distinct types of discipline. Perhaps the most important type is self-discipline. There are also corrective disciplines, preventative disciplines, supportive disciplines, and spiritual disciplines. All of them serve the purpose of developing self-control and meeting a goal.

Self-discipline involves the actions taken to keep oneself focused on reaching one's goals. Self-discipline gives you the qualities needed to stick to difficult tasks. It helps you overcome obstacles and discomfort and pushes yourself to new heights. A man who struggles with anger creates a self-discipline to journal every night. This becomes an outlet for his anger. He also creates a discipline to work out as an outlet for his pent-up energy.

Corrective disciplines are the measures taken when people are not following the rules. Our judicial system uses corrective discipline when they are dealing with lawbreakers. Preventative disciplines are measures that are taken to preempt misbehavior. A parent may set a curfew for their young teen as a preventative discipline for them. There are supportive disciplines to help others stay on or return to their path. A physical therapist in a rehab hospital may give supportive discipline to their patient.

A disciple is a student who studies a discipline. Spiritual discipline is what leads to righteousness. We must become a disciple of Jesus, a student of His teaching. We must discipline ourselves to be more Christlike, allowing the Holy Spirit to make us righteous. Righteousness involves the right behavior and right living.

This is not the natural way that we live because of our sinful nature. We are prone to not thinking or behaving in the right manner. That is, we often initially respond to circumstances in a way that is either self-seeking or harmful toward those around us. This is an undisciplined life. Our immediate responses in words, actions, or thoughts can often be damaging. If you disagree, I encourage you to observe the nature of your immediate thoughts in response to the situations of life. When someone cuts you off on the road or hurls a demeaning comment at you, how do you respond? Typically, our first response is self-focused. We get defensive or lash out. An observation of kids shows this to be true. Tantrums take place out of self-focused desires. This is why parents need to teach kids how to share. People need to be taught how to respond correctly. It is through maturity and discipline that our course of focus is changed. The *how* to live disciplined is a key question for any person. Each person has a diverse set of struggles, so the process and areas of work are different.[31]

If you want to build discipline in your life, you must plan. Any discipline done without a plan is prone to fail. In the plan, there are multiple steps. You can think of them like tools in a toolbox. These tools are envision, strategize, implement and measure, and adjust.[32]

The first tool in the plan is having a vision. You must envision where you want to be. What is the destination? If you do not know where you want to go, you will never arrive. You do not need to know the path yet, but this is fixing your eyes on who you want to be. This is where long-range goals may be set. Make it specific and measurable. A newly diagnosed diabetic envisions themselves shedding that sixty pounds of stubborn weight they have always wanted to lose. They do not know how, but those sixty pounds are coming off!

The next tool is to strategize. This may take some self-reflection and may involve some honest, hard-to-accept truth about yourself. You need to know where you struggle and how you succeed. This will help map out your strategy. You need to analyze past behavior and be honest with yourself about your strengths and weaknesses. We often are not as strong as we think we are. This tool involves setting some short-term and mid-range goals as checkpoints for the strategy. These goals are a set of targets to hit. Make the targets achievable and realistic. Also, in developing your strategy, you must have tactics to help you be successful. This can be a lot of different things. It includes finding supporters to encourage you along the path. It includes removing obstacles and temptations. It may involve changing the way we do things. Those things (behaviors, thoughts, and patterns) that led you to unsatisfactory results in the past need to be changed. Plan some rewards along the way to give added motivation. Create constant reminders of the path you are setting to keep yourself mindful of the journey.

The third tool is implementation and measurement. This is your plan. Execute it. It starts with taking the first step. Start small and own it. Do not wait for it to feel right because that feeling, if it ever comes, is fleeting. You must stick to practicing your plan whether you feel like it or not. This is discipline. Ignore the negative feelings and focus on the positive. Start each day with a commitment to your path. You need ways to measure your progress. If it is a weight goal, take regular measurements (good or bad). If it is a "change the habit" goal, record the length of time since you last indulged and take pride over every day you practice restraint. Understand that you will fail. Do not let it ruin you. Setbacks are normal. Have a plan for when you fall to help you get up and continue forward. Maybe you need to confess your failure to a supporter and then commit to starting again. Building a new discipline means repeating this step over and over.

The last tool is to adjust. Some strategies sound and look great on paper, but then circumstances change, and adjustments are needed. Weather or schedule changes may affect your strategic plan. It may be that as you progress in your journey, habits are forming, and adjustments are needed for increased challenge or change of focus. Jim has been working on his workout plan for months now, and he is getting stronger, but he is getting bored with it. It is time to adjust to a new routine to spark renewed desire and momentum. Paula sees that winter is approaching, and she will need to have another plan if the weather is too cold or snowy for her morning run. Discipline involves adjusting for effectiveness.

Gary struggles with gambling. He has frequently found moments of temptation at convenience-store counters, where he has a tough time leaving without several scratch-off tickets. Gary knows that he feels successful when he avoids counters that sell lottery tickets. He envisions a life lived without the desire to buy scratch tickets. He sets a goal for himself to go a month without buying any lottery tickets. He strategizes with a plan that includes paying at the pump, using self-checkout lines, and having someone go with him to places where he knows he cannot avoid the tickets. Knowing he needs to fill his car the next day, he drives to the station with clear intent not to enter the building where his habit gets fed. He is successful at doing this for the first week. But then an unexpected situation arises, and he needs to drop by the grocery store. While walking past the counter, he sees the lottery ticket vending machine, and his impulse kicks in. "It has been a long time, and I've been really good," he rationalizes. Before even having a chance to call for help, he has bought two tickets and cannot wait to get back to the car to scratch them. Feeling horrible about his failure (and losing $10), he calls and confesses to his support friend, Ralph, and recommits to the plan. Gary is using discipline to change.

DISCIPLINE ACROSS LIFE CHANGES

Discipline has never been a strong characteristic of mine, which makes the thought of writing about it humorous. I have learned a lot about the topic and how to implement it in life. Learning about it and implementing it are two different things. My problem is that my mood and temperament are different every day. This can make disciplined living difficult. Imagine that you commute to work every day; but every day, when you get up, you are leaving from a different location. Some days take longer than others to get there. Some days, it is a short journey to where you want to go. Some days, you just want to call in sick. Discipline helps to regulate yourself. Discipline became a key factor in my life after my world was turned upside down.

After the truth of my offense came out, my life changed quickly and dramatically. With my offense and my move out of the house becoming known to people around me, many things changed. I came to view this as a corrective discipline in my life. It was hard. Though that is the truth, I do not want to paint myself as a victim in any way. The pains from this season were the fallout from my actions. I owned it and accepted it.

Discipline can be hard. Hebrews 12:11 says, "No discipline seems pleasant at the time, but painful. Later on, however, it produces a harvest of righteousness and peace for those who have been trained by it." Effective discipline includes purpose in the pain. The pain should lead to productivity. If discipline does not include some amount of discomfort in your life, it loses out on purpose or productivity. In Guzik's commentary, he encourages those who are disciplined to look at the result instead of the process. Discipline is about what it is going to do for you or what it is intended to produce. Spiritual discipline is not just about a "heavenly spanking" or its temporary unpleasant nature. It is about the harvest of righteousness and peace for those trained by discipline. It is about getting strong, getting right, and getting bold.[33] When that happens, then watch out.

Chastening is to correct by punishment or suffering. Guzik describes discipline as chastening. I would come to experience chastening in the wilderness. I called this season of my life the valley as I reflected on Psalm 23:4. I had officially entered the valley.

My new home became my parents' basement, which was a forty-five-minute drive away from my wife. Marriage is not intended to be lived apart. This led to a new set of disciplines for my wife and me in communication, companionship, and intimacy. Next, I would not be able to attend the church I had been going to with my family for fourteen years. I would need to find a new discipline for getting spiritually fed. One of my prior commitments was drumming as a regular member of the music team. Now, I had to step away from involvement in this group. Additionally, I was a leader in a ministry, and my responsibility was to teach. I had to resign from that post, which affected over one hundred men.

I quickly realized that my failure not only affected me but also hundreds of people from all my involvements. I wish there was a way I could apologize to all of them for the impact it had on them. If I had a complete understanding of the ripple effect and impact it had, I could author an essay more than a hundred pages in length. If every person could understand that everything they do affects other people in some way, it may change the way they behave. You may not see it—and often we do not—but the impact happens. I live near the Twin Cities in Minnesota. As I drive the busy highways during rush hour, it is a constant practice of observation and response. When one person changes lanes, it causes others to slow down to make room. When that happens, the occupants of the exited lane move up to fill in the gap. If a person has pulled over on the side of the road for an emergency, traffic responds by moving over a lane until the vehicle has passed. Every action affects another person in some way.

So the key question in this space was "Now what?" I was on my own with no commitments and greatly diminished responsibilities. I could not go to my home or church. I had no ministry for which to create plans. It felt like incredible freedom on one side but total restraint on the other side. I could do what I wanted, but I could not do what I wanted (be with my wife and kids). I went from being around a lot of people in different settings to being around very few people. God was stretching me during this time. What does a people-oriented person do when they cannot be around people? What does a team player do with no team?

The answer was to work on myself. The process lay in developing discipline. It was what I needed to cling to when it felt all was falling away. If I had not leaned into living a disciplined life, I would have fallen so fast into destructive tendencies. I would have eaten to comfort myself. I would have spent money buying things to excite myself. I would have distracted myself with anything and everything to keep me from facing my circumstances. And all that would have dug the grave deeper. I needed to live disciplined.

I envisioned what I wanted to be. I visualized being back together with my family. (I was thinking six months, not two-plus years.) I saw myself having lost weight. I imagined learning some new skills in all the extra time I now had. I thought of reading books I have accumulated but never took the time to read. Next, I strategized how to do that. I signed up with an app called Noom, which taught me a lot about the psychology behind healthy living. This would be a daily exercise of reading and practicing. I had my wife bring me my bass guitar and amp so I could start practicing. I created a schedule for myself. I put boundaries around my time so I could get everything done in the day. This helped minimize wasted time. I made eating, sleeping, and planning activities goals and incorporated them into the schedule.

I was not perfect, but I grew. I worked on developing habits and being productive. I kept my eyes on the long-term because the short-term was very discouraging (more on this in the next chapter). Reaching little short-term goals helped keep my momentum going. Every little "win" felt good. Setbacks were difficult, emotionally and psychologically, but they taught perseverance.

No person is completely strong enough on their own. My faith and relationship with my Savior, Jesus, was critical at this time. He is the rock I would run to stand on when I felt like I was drowning. The best thing I could do was reach out my hands to Jesus for help. I would pray. I would just be silent. I would think about His attributes and His promises found in the Bible. I found peace in Him.

At first, there were several times a day when I felt so overwhelmed emotionally by the mountain that I was facing that I would weep uncontrollably. Over the first six months, discipline would help me deal with this. I began learning tools to help me in these situations. One of these tools was the "Who I Am in Christ" list found in Neil Anderson's book *Victory over the Darkness*.[15] This was key to shaping how I viewed myself. Next, I learned to identify my supporters and to call for help when feeling low (not always easy to do). It helped to hear a human voice to reassure and uplift me. Music was also a huge help. I had a playlist of music to redirect my thinking. It primarily consisted of godly worship music to turn my focus from self to God. I also received counseling, which helped greatly as well. My wife and I had two wonderful Christian counselors who helped us. All this was helpful because it pointed me back to Jesus.

People may think or feel that following God is too restrictive. "Don't do this" or "You must do this" are the rules of the game. That is a lot of what religion is, and it is meant to help live disciplined and purposeful. Jesus is about more than rules and discipline. Jesus wants a relationship with us. He calls us friend (Luke 5:20). He loves us greatly (1 John 3:1). He has forgiven those who receive Him as Savior (Psalm 103:12). He provides for the needs of His followers (Philippians 4:19). We find peace and joy when we live disciplined lives that are rooted in faith in Jesus.

> *We find peace and joy when we live disciplined lives that are rooted in faith in Jesus.*

JOB

There is a man in the Bible whose identity and life rooted in God also helped him when he went through a time of great loss. His name is Job, and his story is incredible. I have often thought that no matter how bad life can seem, there is always someone who has it worse. It is hard to imagine a life tougher than what Job encountered. It all unfolds in the first thirty-two verses of this Old Testament book.

Job is described as blameless and upright. He feared (respected) God and shunned evil. Job was a good man. Job was greatly blessed and had great wealth. He had seven sons and three daughters. He owned seven thousand sheep, three thousand camels, five hundred yoke of oxen, and five hundred donkeys. He had many servants. He was the greatest man among all the people of the East (Job 1:1–3). Job was sitting pretty, and life was good—that is, until Satan went to the Lord.

Job 1:7 says, "Satan came before the Lord and was questioned where he has been." He responded that he had been roaming throughout the earth. The Lord asked him if he had considered His servant Job. After some back-and-forth dialogue, the Lord allowed everything that Job had to be put under the power of Satan (Job 1:12) but not to lay a finger on Job himself. What happens next is what you should expect from Satan.

Satan is a lying snake who is out to steal, kill, and destroy (John 10:10). Job's life was altered by an "earthquake." Everything Job had was lost. All his eleven thousand animals were either stolen or destroyed. Then, his ten children were killed when their houses collapsed on them. Job responded with incredible grief but also incredible spiritual discipline when he said, "Naked I came from my mother's womb, and naked I will depart. The Lord gave and the Lord has taken away; may the name of the Lord be praised" (Job 1:21). He did not blame God with wrongdoing. He did not curse at God and lose faith. In his anguish, he kept a discipline of respect for his Lord.

That is not where it stops, though. Job 2 starts with Satan again going before the Lord. The same dialogue went back and forth before the Lord again suggested His servant Job. In verse 6, Job's physical life was put in the control of Satan, who was told to spare his life. Immediately, Satan afflicted Job with painful sores from the soles of his feet to the crown of his head. His belief was that Job would now curse God. To help with this goal, Job's wife (probably influenced by Satan) encouraged him to "curse God and die!" (Job 2:9). I am fairly sure that Job's wife was dealing with her own grief as well. Again, Job's spiritual discipline kicked in when he responded, "Shall we accept good from God, and not trouble?"

It is normal for people to blame God when calamity hits. We question *why* so many things do not go as we would want them. It is as if we expect life to be all sunshine and roses. God has never promised a pain-free life for anyone. He tells us the opposite. Jesus told us that we would have trouble in this life (John 16:33). Job presents a great question for us to consider. We certainly accept the good things that God blesses us with, but shouldn't we also accept the "trouble" we experience? Living through trouble is what helps us grow and discipline us to be more Christlike.

The story of Job continues for forty more chapters as Job had conversations with friends who had come to "help." Amid these conversations, you can hear the disciplines of Job's beliefs that helped make him the "upright and blameless" man he is described to be. In chapter 18, Job's friend Bildad tried to convince Job that he must have done something wicked because God punishes the wicked. Job refuted this, and he said, "I know that my redeemer lives, and that in the end he will stand on the earth. And after my skin has been destroyed, yet in my flesh I will see God" (Job 19:25–26). His confidence was in the Lord. In chapter 22, Job's friend Eliphaz contended the same manner of Job's wickedness. Job countered by saying, "I have not departed from the commands of his lips; I have treasured the words of his mouth more than my daily bread" (Job 23:12).

Discipline involves living out what you believe. Job is contending that trouble does not necessarily come because you have not been true to what you believe in. Life is filled with lessons to be learned, and the challenging times teach us more quickly and effectively than the good times do. Sometimes having our cage rattled gets our attention more than a shout. God is sovereign. He allows things to happen to make us better people. He lets us suffer pain to remind us of our need for Him. We must believe that God is good, even when life is not good.

The book of Job ends in an amazing way. This shows the power of God that I place my faith and trust in. He *is able* to restore what is lost. In chapter 42, Job prayed for his friends, and amends were made for their words spoken against the Lord to Job (Job 42:7). Then, "after Job had prayed for his friends, the Lord restored his fortunes and gave him twice as much as he had before" (Job 42:10). "The Lord blessed the latter part of Job's life more than the former part. He had 14,000 sheep, 6,000 camels, 1,000 yoke of oxen, and 1,000 donkeys [That is twenty-two thousand animals!] He also had seven sons and three daughters" (Job 42:12–13).

There is an unwritten piece from Job's story that I see when I read between the lines. What do you do when you lose everything like Job did? It would be easy to admit defeat and give up. Most of us would complain to anyone and everyone about what life has dealt us with. But that is living undisciplined. There is nothing but defeat in that type of thinking. I do not believe that Job lived like that. Sure, he grieved his losses, and that probably took some time. But eventually, discipline led him to get up and start over. That is where you must go. You must believe that you are not done until all your days are up and that we do not know when our days will be up, so we must keep going. In the end, Job's life was restored to an even greater place than before.

DISCIPLINE LEADS TO RENEWED HOPE

Job did not give up on God, and he was restored. There was never a promise that would happen, but he had a discipline of belief and confidence in the Lord. When you trust and make room in your life for God to act, He will. Be assured, though, that He acts in His perfect timing. He is a loving, caring, restoring God, who desires, above all, for us to become the people He designed us to be. Living disciplined helps you arrive at that place. It takes high-octane discipline to keep you fueled on the road to restoration.

My journey in the valley was about enacting discipline for the road ahead. I did not know where this whole journey would take me, but I knew I would not be alone. For now, it was about living in a new normal and seeking the Lord for His guidance. A huge part of this section of the valley was identifying, learning about, and getting rid of the garbage thinking that had made its way into my life. You could call it an unmaking.

There is a favorite song from 2015 that God reminded me of one day. It is a song that addresses the process of unlearning the harmful parts of life and replacing them with truth that grows us to be what we were created to be. The song is called "The Unmaking," and it was written by Nichole Nordeman and David Hodges:[34]

> This is the unmaking
> Beauty and the breaking
> Had to lose myself to find out who you are
> Before each beginning

> There must be an ending
> Sitting in the rubble
> I can see the stars
> This is the unmaking.

The unmaking is painful and hard to go through. Although it is part of the valley, we do not walk alone. The enemy wants us to believe we walk alone. He wants us to believe that we have no future. We are good enough on our own. Healing comes when we get ourselves—our faulty thoughts and our self-centered focus—out of the way. God tells us that He will never leave us or forsake us. He sends His Holy Spirit to His followers to fulfill that promise. Our future is bright. We can have hope. Live disciplined.

PERSONAL QUESTIONS

1. How do you view discipline?

2. How have you experienced discipline in your life?

3. What disciplines do you need to get yourself up when life has you down?

4. How do you need to be unmade in your life?

We find peace and joy when we live disciplined lives that are rooted in faith in Jesus.

Chapter 9
LIVING IN THE UNKNOWN

> May the God of hope fill you with all joy and peace as you trust in Him, so that you may overflow with hope by the power of the Holy Spirit.
>
> —Romans 15:13

HOPE

It is a beautiful, sunny day, and John sits at the window and stares out into the small yard in front of the house where he just arrived. John is a wiry ten-year-old boy who just arrived at his fourth house in three weeks. He has been in and out of foster homes, looking for a more permanent place. He does not know either of his parents. His father left long before he was born, and his mother could not support him and her addictions. His original adoptive family turned out to be abusive, leaving him where he is now. As he stares out the window, he wonders how long he will be there and what will come next. Will he get along with this new family, or will they move him on as well?

Juanita is a teenage young woman from Haiti whose life has been anything but easy. Her dad left to go to work and provide for the family when she was a baby, but he never returned. Her home has been destroyed three times because of hurricanes, and her current home is only temporary and houses ten different families. Her mom tries to work, but work is hard to find. Juanita has not been to school for years because she needs to take care of her two brothers. She does her best to help, but she often feels inadequate. Is this all there is in life? Is there anything to look forward to? She feels stuck in a situation with no hope for the future.

Steve is a lawyer in Ohio who worked extremely hard to get to where he is today. He has his own practice and has built a solid reputation around the city. Steve has a beautiful home with his wife of twenty-eight years, and there is not a comfort in life that he does not get to enjoy. Steve's three kids have grown and are doing well themselves. He is proud of them and what they have accomplished, but he finds himself wishing they would call or come by more often. Over the last few years, Steve has had a growing sense of emptiness in his work. He wonders if he makes a difference in the world around him. He often wonders why he does not feel more content with his life.

You could tell story after story of people whose lives are filled with questions about their existence. Is there more to life than this? Am I doing any good? What purpose does my life have? The answers lie in where you place your hope. Hope helps to find fulfillment. Hope tells them there is something better ahead. Hope carries you through the unknown. It is a key component of one's life.

> *Hope carries you through the unknown.*

Hope is both a noun and a verb. Hope is a desire accompanied by an expectation for something that will fulfill you. It is living with expectancy. "I have hope that he will stick to the plan." "I have hope that the issue will be resolved." Hope is also an action that motivates you. "I am hoping that the plan works out." "I am hoping that the result is favorable." Faith and hope are commonly intertwined because both often involve something that is out of your control. You can plan and organize and prepare to a great extent, but the results require faith and hope.

Hope is often sought after but is a concept often misunderstood. Hope is something deep down in our souls where we place our trust. Hope is much more than simple wishes. It is more than "I hope he gets home on time." It is the very thing that can motivate us to get up in the morning. It can give us the drive to press on. You may say, "My hope is in _____" or "I have *this* hope." What is *this*? What gives you hope for your life? What helps you think that there must be better things to come? What happens when something is done either to you or because of you that severely damages your outlook of hope? What happens when that relationship is fractured or that job is lost or that person dies who played a part in your hope story? Where do you go from there?

"What happens when?" The conclusion of that question can be finished with many issues people face. Regardless of what you finish it with, it is a question to which you should have an answer. How do you proceed? Where do you get the answers? The answer should be found where your hope is placed.

People place their hope in many things. Some people place their hope in money. Millions of dollars are spent each year on lottery tickets, hoping for that big payday. Or if they could just get that raise, it would solve all the problems. Some people place their hope in other people. Spouses are given the expectation of being the one to "complete" us. But just as quickly, they are blamed for the lack of contentment in life. As I have mentioned previously, we are all dealing with a sin problem we cannot resolve. Money cannot save us from this problem. Other people cannot save us. We are all rowing the same boat (called the USS Sinful Nature). Hope in other people is futile. Money and other people are two common places where hope is placed, and the list could go on. Each of them eventually fails to satisfy.

There is only one reliable and solid foundation a person should place their hope. A foundation that cannot be shaken. A foundation that has been around since the existence of time. Actually, He is the creator of time. He is the backbone of this book. His name is Jesus. Jesus is the cornerstone upon which you can build your life. He is your hope for all time. He is the firm foundation (2 Timothy 2:19). He is the only hope for overcoming the sin problem with which you and I are infected. Placing your hope in anything else is like building on sand.

Jesus spoke about foundations like sand in Matthew 7:24–27. Those who listen to His words and follow them are building their house—think hope—on a firm foundation. Those who choose to trust in something or someone else, including themselves, are like foolish people who build their house (hope) on the sand. The rain comes, and the sand moves, and the house collapses because of the weak foundation. Jesus has given us valuable instructions on how to live and the benefits of finding your hope in him. We find this hope when we place our faith in allowing God to direct our lives. We renew this hope when we read the Bible and spend time daily praying and seeking His guidance.

Finding your hope in Jesus is like finding ripe, juicy fruit from the tree. Scientists at the University of Minnesota developed the honey crisp apple. This type of apple is amazingly juicy and crisp. It is the best-tasting apple I have ever had. It is the best. It reminds me of the fruit that is developed from believers placing their hope in Jesus. This fruit is love, joy, peace, patience, kindness, goodness, faithfulness, gentleness, and self-control (Galatians 5:22). I like being around people who exhibit these attributes.

Finding hope in Jesus has a profound impact on your life. The weight of worry and anxiety falls off when you are finding your hope in Jesus because you know that through Him and in Him, we can do all things (Philippians 4:13). Your eyes are redirected when you trust that God wants the best for you. He has a hope and a future for you, not to harm you but to prosper you (Jeremiah 29:11). Of course, His ideas of what this looks like are often different than what you may want or expect. But you better believe that His ideas of prospering are better than yours.

The truth is that we all can fall prey to looking to a multitude of other things for hope. But other things are just mirages or sources of deception and doubt—the oldest tricks of the enemy. It is easier to trust in what you know and see. It is easier to trust in what you can control. It is easier to trust in yourself. This is the battle for every believer, and it arises when dealing with the unknown. Jesus promises to never leave us or forsake us (Hebrews 13:5). This gives me the assurance of where to place my hope. If you trust that God, the creator of all things, is with you, why would you ever look for fulfillment in anything else? Knowing that He is trustworthy and faithful to His promise, why would you hope for anything else? Nothing else satisfies.

QUESTIONS WITHOUT ANSWERS

Imagine that you are staying the night at a friend's house, and you wake up in the night needing to use the bathroom. You do not want to turn on the light to see the way, so you stumble in the direction of the bathroom. About halfway to the door, your foot discovers the edge of the dresser. This unpleasant discovery causes a whimper to escape your mouth. You gather yourself and make it to the bathroom before returning to resume the night's sleep. You think to yourself that you could make that walk blindfolded at home without issue.

Unknown paths are hard and can often include the pain that comes with unexpected twists and turns. You may know the destination or the anticipated next stop, but how you will get there is a mystery. What will you encounter along the way? How is this-or-that problem going to be overcome? How long is it going to take? Where is this going to take you? Who can help you with all your questions? These are some of the questions I was asking during life in the valley.

The future of my life was littered with numerous unknowns. These unknowns involved timing, support, legal issues, and finances, among many more. There was no roadmap for the trip I was going to be on for the foreseeable future. There was no how-to book written for my situation.

I had mentioned before that my initial thought was that I would be back home within six months. That was severely naive and shorter than reality, but I did not know. The future path and timing were all unknown. I am very appreciative of the hundreds of people who helped my wife and kids during this time. That list is very lengthy, praise the Lord. On the other side, my list was short. The people who knew of my situation were few. How would people respond if they knew? I did not know, and I feared it. I have struggled with letting people's thoughts about me (or at least my perception of those thoughts) affect my self-worth. It was a controlling vice I had to overcome. This led to lonely nights in the valley. (I hung a sign on my bedroom door that said "The Valley" to remind me where I was at.)

After a month had passed, I received a letter that rocked my world. It was a letter with the header *State of Minnesota v. Brian Goodwin*. I stared at that letter for an hour, letting the fear grow inside me. What did this mean? Was I going to prison? What did I need to do? I have never been in this situation. It announced my first court hearing two months from then. I had to wait that long? This was going to eat me up. Within forty-eight hours, I realized that I needed a lawyer. How much does a lawyer cost, and how would we pay for it? This involved a "smorgasbord" of unknowns.

Hindsight is twenty-twenty. As I look back, it is always easier to see life with clarity than when you are in the middle of it. In the middle of a set of circumstances, it is often hard to see the forest for the trees. What makes it seem so hard is the unknown. It is like playing a golf course for the first time. You do not have a clear idea of what the terrain is like up ahead because it is all new to you. You shoot in the right direction and hope that your ball ends up in a favorable position for the next shot. Not knowing what is coming up next or what to expect can make life frustrating and difficult. Every step in the valley was taken with my head on a swivel, looking left and right, looking out in anticipation of what might come. This was emotionally and physically exhausting.

I am not ashamed to say that I cried every single night for the first six months. I felt alone even though I had parents living upstairs. I shamed myself endlessly and struggled with constant negative self-talk. I felt like a victim but knew I was anything but that. I was an instigator receiving his consequences. I did not want to admit that I was depressed. I have known too many people who wave that "depression" flag around, trying to garner attention. I did not want to be that person, so I kept my thoughts inside. That is an unhealthy thing to do. Isolation is a dangerous place when you are depressed. My wife and I talked each night about not much in particular. The first six months were difficult, and I knew I needed help. I was being stretched in uncomfortable ways and challenged in life. Would I look inward to find hope, or would I live my faith out by trusting Jesus? I knew the answer was to turn to Jesus in hope.

I trusted God. I trusted that nothing surprised Him. I trusted that He had a plan. I had confessed and repented months prior, although that does not mean that I would be spared from consequences. Forgiveness from God is promised, but freedom from earthly consequences is not. Still, I had hope that the Holy Spirit, who is a promise to every believer, would be with me, helping me along the path of the unknown. The Holy Spirit would comfort me in my unknowns. This hope would be my firm foundation each night when fear and anxiety would creep in. Calling on the name of Jesus and asking for the Holy Spirit within me to arise would bring me peace and hope that passes understanding (Philippians 4:7).

RUTH

There is a character in the Old Testament who experienced many unknowns in her life. Like many women, Ruth grew up longing for a husband, family, and probably a good life. She surely rejoiced when she married Kilion. It did not bother her that he was an Israelite, and she was a Moabite. She had future thoughts about her kids to come. Her dreams ran wild. That all changed unexpectedly. The unexpected is usually a front-runner for the unknown.

Ruth comforted Kilion when his father had died ten years prior. That was hard on him. Now, Ruth was the one needing comfort because her husband and his brother had died. Overnight, she and her sister-in-law, Orpah, joined her mother-in-law, Naomi, as widows. "Now, what do we do?" she asked. Naomi would ask the Lord, "Is this punishment from God for leaving the land promised to our ancestors and marrying outside of our nation?" Orpah would ask Naomi, "How will we survive?" Life quickly became riddled with unknowns.

Naomi decided to go back to the land of Judah, where she had come from. She knew this would mean going to a foreign country for her daughters-in-law, so she instructed them to go back to their mother's home and pray for the Lord to show kindness. She advised that there would be a better chance for them to remarry back in their hometowns. They all had a decision to make. Forks in the road are usually filled with unknowns. Often, one path is wide and easy. The other is narrow and rough. Which one would these daughters choose? Orpah decided to go home and kissed Naomi goodbye, but Ruth decided to go with Naomi (Ruth 1:14). After some questioning, Naomi relented, and they set off for Judah.

I've often envisioned Ruth as a shy and quiet head-turner. When they arrived in Bethlehem in Judah, one of the first jobs was to find some food. Fortunately for them, it was harvesttime. On that day, it was customary for field owners to leave a remnant behind as the field was harvested. This was meant for the poor and needy to come and glean (pick up the leftovers). In fact, if the harvesters accidentally dropped a bundle, they were instructed not to pick it up. Knowing this, Ruth suggested to Naomi that she go and glean in the fields. She chose a field owned by Boaz.

As chance happened, or possibly divine appointment, Boaz stopped by that day and noticed Ruth gleaning. When he asked who she was, his overseer told Boaz that she was from Moab and had returned with Naomi. Hearing this news, Boaz spoke to Ruth and instructed her to only glean from his field. He instructed his men to protect her and provide for her. He had heard of her faithfulness to Naomi and wanted to bless her. If she was thirsty, there was water for her. At mealtime, Boaz called for her and gave her some roasted grain. He instructed some sheaves of harvested grain be left for her. Boaz took care of Ruth. If fear and anxiety were part of Ruth's unknown, they were dealt a blow by Boaz's generosity.

Ruth returned home that evening and blew Naomi's mind with the quantity of goods she possessed. Inquiring about where she found herself, Ruth dropped the name of Boaz, and this lit Naomi up. "That man is our close relative; he is one of our guardian-redeemers" (Ruth 2:20). That was a big deal in those days. It was a hope builder. It was an answer to an unknown. To whom would they turn? Where could they turn? The fire of hope had been ignited.

Hope leads one to action. This is the case for Ruth and Naomi. Naomi always had Ruth's future in mind, even if the *how* was unknown. With Boaz providing for Ruth, Naomi saw an opportunity. Now, the way this plays out is kind of foreign in our place and time, but what ensues is like a marriage proposal from Ruth toward Boaz. She was instructed to stalk him until he went to sleep, then go lie down next to him at his feet. When he would ask who it was, she would tell him and do what he said. She followed the instructions; and in the middle of the night, Boaz noticed her and, upon asking, found that it was Ruth. He was taken aback by her approach. He was amazed that she had chosen him instead of one of the younger stallions around the area. He sent her home with more barley, a promise, and a bucket full of hope. He would attend to the matter the next day.

The guardian-redeemer is a person who is responsible for safeguarding a family's property, including people, when tragedy strikes. The lineage of Elimelech (Naomi's husband) was on course to perish since both of his sons had died. Naomi needed a guardian-redeemer (some translations say *kinsman-redeemer*) to redeem what was lost. Ruth was part of the property to be redeemed if Boaz would agree. Boaz knew of a closer guardian-redeemer than him, so the property was offered to that man first but with the condition that that man would have to take Ruth as his wife. That was a deal-breaker for the closer redeemer, and so Boaz was granted the chance. He accepted his role and was married to Ruth.

HOPE IN THE UNKNOWN

The story of Ruth is a story filled with unknowns that were supplied with hope. Ruth trusted Naomi, who trusted God to provide. God provided the restoration to Elimelech's lineage. The result is a small section of the genealogy that led, first, to King David in three generations and ultimately to Jesus.

Our unknowns are opportunities to hope and trust. That is a key perspective change that had to happen in my life. Just like driving behind an 18-wheeler that you cannot see around, it is hard not to know what is coming ahead. It is hard not being in control and being forced out of your way of doing things. But if we are placing our hope in ourselves and our choices, disappointment is usually up ahead. Seek the Lord and place your hope in Him and His ways. Read His guidebook, pray, and trust. The stress of the unknowns will feel a lot lighter. You will have more confidence; and someday, looking in the rearview mirror, you will see clearly what was done. I had to learn this lesson, and it took some time. Hoping in myself gets me nowhere. Hoping in Jesus moves me forward and allows Him to work on me.

There is a song written by Benjamin Hastings, Dylan Thomas, and

Joel Houston called "Know You Will."³⁵ It was performed by Hillsong United. The lyrics were a confidence booster for me when the unknowns tried to drag me down. They reflect the hope and trust that we can have in our Sovereign God.

> I don't know how You'll make a way, but I know You will.
> You've been good on every promise from Eden to Zion
> Through every dead end, and out of that grave
> I don't know how You'll make a way, but I know You will.

In the unknowns, we must place our hope in Jesus Christ. He sees the beginning and the end and is able to help. From our vantage point, we may not know how He will make a way, but with our faith and our hope placed in Him, we know that He will do something amazing with our lives.

PERSONAL QUESTIONS

1. What comes to mind when you hear the word *hope*?

2. Who or what do you place your hope in when times get tough? What examples of hope-placing do you have in your life?

3. How do you find it difficult to place your hope in the Lord?

4. Read the story of Ruth. It is four short chapters. How does her life challenge and encourage you?

Hope carries you through the unknown.

Chapter 10
MAKING LEMONADE

> May God Himself, the God of peace, sanctify you through and through. May your whole spirit, soul, and body be kept blameless at the coming of our Lord Jesus Christ.
>
> —1 Thessalonians 5:23

PATIENCE

There are several moments in a person's life that come with incredible anticipation. The sixteen-year-old who cannot wait to get their driver's license. The high school senior who cannot wait to graduate. The vacationer whose departure date is days away. I am convinced that, somehow, time slows down during the waiting period. Days seem to become longer as the event approaches. Early May of 2003 was such a time for my wife and me.

In the summer of 2002, my wife greeted me after work with first-time news that no one forgets. I was going to be a father. We had anticipated it, and so I was not shocked, but hearing that for the first time was momentous. Fast-forward to May, the time was almost here. The due date came and went with no activity, not odd for firstborns. We waited anxiously. The night of May 16, I had come to bed to meet my wife, who had been there much earlier. She announced that the pains had commenced. Oh my, the excitement and the panic! We had prepared, but it was just that until now. Time to put the plan into action. I called my boss and notified him I would not be in to work the next day. He was aware it was coming.

Now, growing up, I was taught that this moment would involve rushing to the car and driving ninety miles per hour, weaving between cars to get to the hospital. Isn't that what the movies portrayed? That was not what happened. We called the hospital to let them know we would be coming. They asked my wife a few questions and then gave directions, which resulted in several hours before needing to make that drive. No high-speed driving for me. At about five the next morning, it was time to go. There was not a lot of sleep for either of us that night. When we arrived at the hospital, we waited some more. Eventually, the room came open, and my wife was instructed to "get comfortable" while waiting even more. I got the music playing (I still remember what I put on) to help calm my wife and settle in the room. The nurses got her all hooked up for monitoring, but waiting was the game we were playing. Our firstborn arrived at ten that night of May 17. A full twenty-four hours had passed, and the waiting seemed endless but worth it. Kobe Brian Goodwin was introduced into the world, and it was a significant, life-changing occasion. One of the most incredible moments of my life. I gained a new title that night: father. A title one cannot take lightly. A moment I had expectantly waited for my whole life was here. A virtue that followed along this journey was one called patience.

Patience is expectant waiting while remaining calm. It is what is needed when you are sitting at the red light, and you are running late for an appointment. It is what is needed when you are ready for that dinner date, and your date is not on the same timetable as you are. It is what is needed when your sales pitch is presented flawlessly, but the buyer is not sure yet.

Patience can be gut-wrenching at times because it often involves dealing with situations out of our control. You have put the ball in play on the other side of the court, and you are ready for it to come back to you. But you wait. And you wait some more. All the while, having patience means you are keeping cool. Your emotions remain steady and calm. Your countenance is as smooth as a lake on a still day. This sounds like it is easy, but patience is often not easy.

Control is something that people like to possess. We have an idea of how it should be done, and we want it done our way. When something prevents that from happening, we tend to get impatient. We do not like to wait, and we get agitated when we do. Patience says, "Just hold on a moment. There may be a better way, and it may not be yours." Sometimes patience reminds you that people are not always running at the same speed as you are. They just need a little more time. Maybe you need to slow down.

In a children's movie entitled *The Music Machine*, there is a song entitled "Patience," and it is sung by Herbert the Snail.[36] This song teaches important lessons about patience. The following is the chorus:

> Have patience, Have patience.
> Don't be in such a hurry.
> When you get impatient, you only start to worry.
> Remember, remember that God is patient, too.
> And think of all the times when others have to wait for you.

What happens when you get impatient? There is a host of physiological things that happen in one's body when dealing with impatience. Perhaps you can think of a time when you were impatient and can recall these occurring. The song says you start to worry. That is a start. Besides that, your body warms up and tenses up, and you begin to sweat. Your breathing can become shallow and speed up. You often become irritable, snappy, and anxious. Impatience is often at the root of your stress in life. It can lead to rash decisions and poor behavior.

Impatience (im-patience) sounds like a lack of patience. However, it is the other way around. Impatience is a very particular physical process that gets triggered under specific circumstances. It often motivates specific kinds of decisive action. Patience is really a shadow term signifying a lack of impatience. Patience is overcoming the impatience that naturally arises in your life.[37]

Patience requires a plan. Impatience is a natural reaction to specific circumstances, so you need to have a plan to handle it when it surfaces. As with many other natural reactions in your life, recognition is often the first part of the plan. Like a coach who calls a time-out when the team starts to fall apart on the court, you need to pause when impatience flares up. Remove yourself from the "court" if you can and take a breather. Once you are there, consider these strategies for curbing your impatience:[38]

1. Breath! Take slow, deep breaths and count to ten. This will slow your heart rate and relax your body. It also begins to distance you from the situation.
2. Scan your body. Mentally assess yourself from your toes to your nose and focus on relaxing.
3. Change your thoughts. Choose to embrace patience and find a way to make the waiting more productive. Think more flexibly. If you want to change your life, change your thoughts.
4. Speak positively to yourself. Use positive statements, such as "I got this" or "It's going to be okay," to help change your mindset.
5. Listen to your body. The cause of your impatience may be your body telling you that it needs fuel or hydration. Eat a snack or drink some water.

Patience is a by-product of the Holy Spirit residing in you. It is a "fruit" that grows on a person who professes Jesus Christ as their Lord and Savior. This fruit is described in Galatians 5:22. Some translations call this forbearance, which involves self-controlled restraint. Understanding the forgiveness that is offered to every person reframes our perspective. It causes humility. When we understand that Christ, who has every reason to be impatient and upset at our lack of faith in Him, forgives us and loves us unconditionally, we will live differently. We will view those things, which would have triggered us before, as opportunities to grow and be more reflective toward others of Jesus's patience toward us. Patience involves selflessness.

PATIENCE ON THE PATH

During my time in the valley, I was constantly encountering the unknown, as I addressed in the last chapter. So many questions and not many answers. Dealing with the unknown will drive you out of your mind unless you approach it with a proper perspective. When you are walking through the wilderness, you need something to drive toward. It is easy to focus on what you are missing. It is better to focus on what is possible. This mindset became a turning point during my trip to the valley.

I chose to get intentional about the use of my time. I saw that I had an opportunity to grow. I had an opportunity to gain new skills and knowledge that I was not afforded at the time when life was filled with commitments. I became purposeful about how I spent my days. I made measurable goals with specific timeframes. I made plans filled with steps to accomplish what I wanted to do. I set a schedule for myself. The result was growth and a healthier way to live.

Life became purposeful with my designed tasks. For instance, I have wanted to focus on losing some weight for a long time but never really invested the time and attention to make it a reality. So I started a program to teach myself about the psychology of eating. I began making weekly meal plans and learning to bake and cook new meals. I also had several books that I have wanted to read but never had the time to spend. I challenged myself to read a chapter a day and take time to dissect what I took in. I enjoy self-improvement books, and this was helpful in the new thinking I was trying to develop. I listened only to music that was positive in nature, which helped my general mood and outlook on life.

My demeanor and outlook on life began to change. For the first six months or so, there was a great deal of sadness, shaming, and negativity in my thinking. As I took more ownership of my time and intentionality, positivity began to grow. The goals I set slowly started to be achieved. My nights of crying myself to sleep began to change into more restful nights. My relationship with my wife began to improve as we started some counseling together with some outstanding counselors. Change was happening, but it took patience. I was learning how to "make lemonade" with the circumstances of my life.

When you are working on changing something, it can never happen soon enough. Impatience was a real battle because things were not happening as quickly as I wanted. The hearings for the lawsuit against me were three months apart at a time. All the unknown engulfed in this unmapped-out process demanded patience. What was around the upcoming bend on the path was not known, and I had to live in that space.

I began a counseling treatment program, which required homework to be done. The list was long, so I dived into getting them done. It was part of the path to reunifying my family. Each assignment had to be presented in treatment. With the number of people in the group, this translated to every-other-week presentations. This was not fast enough for me. I was driven to complete them, whereas others were not. It required patience.

Patience leads to growth and learning. Life causes you to slow down or just plain stop at times. Matthew McConaughey wrote a book called *Greenlights* that talks about this phenomenon. They are the yellow and red lights of life. In these moments, if you seize the moment and make productive use of this time (as much as you can), you can experience growth and learn much about yourself.[39] I had to learn how to not defeat myself through my thoughts. I had to learn how to recognize the spiritual attacks of the enemy and to differentiate the various "voices" or thoughts I was having.

Every person is born with a conscious voice in their head. We are born with a sinful nature, which, by default, taints our conscious thoughts in a negative way. It may lead you to think things like "I want to eat this food" or "I'm going to go to that place." You think these things even though you are aware both thoughts are against how you really want to live. This voice can be trained somewhat but often needs boundaries to keep it in check. I had to learn to recognize the thoughts I was honoring and what they were leading my mind to believe.

There are two other originators of thought or voices to contend with. These two voices counter each other. Both are spiritual. One is purposed to steal and destroy life from us (John 10:10). This is the voice of the enemy (Satan) or "thief" because he comes to deceptively steal the joy in our lives. The other is a helper (John 14:26) tasked with guiding you in life. The enemy instills thoughts that lead to destruction, such as lies, judgment of others, and other condemning thoughts. The helper, or Holy Spirit, is a gift of God to help us and guide us in victory. The guidance you receive from this voice comes in thoughts supported by love, peace, joy, goodness, kindness, faithfulness, gentleness, and self-control (Galatians 5:22). The guidance is found by way of patience.

I had to learn to determine if my thoughts were being directed by my self-focused desires derived from my sinful nature, or by the forces of the enemy trying to destroy me, or by the Holy Spirit living within me to guide me in victorious, God-honoring thoughts and living. If you do not deal with a wrestling match in your thoughts, you may need to discern if you are allowing the Holy Spirit to have a voice in your life or not. The enemy, despising Jesus and hating His followers, will be present to disrupt growth in your spiritual relationship. The battle always starts in the mind. If you still do not sense the battle between these two spiritual forces, seek the Holy Spirit and ask Him to reveal where deceptive thoughts are influencing you. The enemy is crafty and deceitful. Sometimes good things can be twisted to be destruction in disguise.

The valley was a God-ordained time of self-improvement. I wanted it to pass quickly, but God's ways are not my ways. I had to have patience because he was doing work on me and stretching me in ways I needed to be stretched. He was teaching me lessons involving the "lemons" in my life. It was a time of humility. It was a time of trusting the Lord. It was a time of staying open-minded to needed change. The lemonade was good, but patience made it even better. Patience is vital when navigating the road of restoration.

> *Patience is vital when navigating the road of restoration.*

NEHEMIAH AND JERUSALEM REBUILD

In the Old Testament, the books of Ezra and Nehemiah detail a story of restoration. More than four hundred years before the birth of Jesus, the city of Jerusalem was conquered by the Babylonians, who destroyed the city and exiled its people to Babylon. God had issued judgment on the Israelites' unfaithfulness to Him and their worship of other gods. Jerusalem lay broken down in rubble. It became a ghost town. The exiled might have wondered where God was in all this. Why would He allow this to happen? Would He act?

This seems to be common for most restoration stories. Focus is taken off the one true God, and worship of other gods leads to brokenness and depravity. Maybe your life feels broken down because some other god has taken over your life and left you exiled from the life you wish you could be living. The god of our life is that which we give the most time, attention, and resources. Maybe we find ourselves worshipping our jobs or another person or that thing that consumes us. Most of the time, we do not mean to shift our attention. It just happens because we do not intentionally guard ourselves against it. It is usually a slow fade toward worshipping something else. Eventually, we may find the error of our ways (after we lose our job, the person leaves, or the thing breaks). When this happens, the appropriate response is to turn from our wrong choices, repent, and seek our Lord and Savior Jesus. He is faithful, loving, and forgiving to those who choose Him. He is able to fix what we break. It may not be immediate, but He can restore it. But you must have patience.

For the Israelites, it took patience. Regarding Jerusalem, seventy-some years later, some of the exiles are allowed to return to their homeland to settle again. Only a small fraction of the exiled returned; and for a long time, the temple, the walls, and the gates remained in ruin. In the book of Ezra, the temple was rebuilt; and a spiritual foundation was laid once again for Israel, God's chosen people. Then comes the story of Nehemiah.

The book of Nehemiah begins fifteen years after the book of Ezra ends. This is almost one hundred years after the first captives came back to the Promised Land and about 150 years after the city of Jerusalem was destroyed. Prior to this, the citizens of Jerusalem had tried to rebuild the walls but had failed. In Ezra 4:6–23, we see that some Israelites tried to rebuild the walls but were stopped by their enemies. Without the walls being rebuilt, Jerusalem would be an easy target for any nation wanting to destroy the Israelites. As the book of Nehemiah begins, the poor condition of the walls and gates was made known to Nehemiah (Nehemiah 1:3).

Nehemiah was someone important. He was a cupbearer who lived in the palace in the capital city of the Persians, and he had access to the king. Hearing the bad report of the town of his ancestors brought him sadness. A side note regarding this: Nehemiah had most likely never been to Jerusalem and probably had never even met any of the people who had returned. One may wonder why he would have such compassion. I believe that Nehemiah had a heart for the things of God. The history of this great city, his ancestors, and the promises of God hooked him. His reaction in Nehemiah 1:4 reflects this compassion. It says that Nehemiah "sat down and wept." For many days, he mourned, fasted, and prayed.

Guzik's commentary states a phenomenal observation. Guzik says, "God was going to do something about this situation. But first, God did something in Nehemiah. Any great work of God begins with God doing a great work in somebody."[40] Nehemiah's heart was right. His desires were pure. He was open to God's leading. This is evident in the prayer found in Nehemiah 1:4–11. He did not have the whole picture in front of him, but he had a restoring, faithful God behind him.

Chapter 2 opens with Nehemiah recounting the encounter with the king that became the springboard for his mission. He was delivering the wine to the king when Nehemiah's sadness was recognized, and he was asked about it. "What do you want?" the king asked (Nehemiah 2:4). This is such a basic and foundational question. A question we should ask ourselves and seek an answer to. A question that Nehemiah had an answer for. He wanted to rebuild. He wanted letters to provide safe conduct for transit. He wanted a letter to Asaph for resources. It is important to identify what we want and need and take that, first, before the Lord and, second, before someone who can help make it happen. Then, we trust in God and His timing. It was good that Nehemiah did this because his wishes were granted, and he was free to go rebuild.

Nehemiah 2:11–15 details the results of the initial inspection of the walls. It was bad, and the work was going to be extensive. This mountain of a project was going to require patience to scale it. Nehemiah knew he would not be able to do the work alone. He had to get help. Too many of us try to take on immense work on our own strength and might. Then we burn out. We lose momentum because we are alone. Nehemiah went to the Jews, the priests, the nobles, and the officials and "told them about the gracious hand of God on him" (Nehemiah 2:18). Together, they replied, "Let us start rebuilding." If you have a mountain-sized problem in front of you, it always helps to have a group of supporters to be together. If you are going *to get there*, you must be *together*.

There will be opposition to anything you set out to do. This is almost a certainty. Nehemiah encountered this throughout the whole rebuilding process, and the opposition grew in intensity as time passed. At first, it was merely questioning. "What is this you are doing?" they were asked (Nehemiah 2:19). Then, it was planned action. "They all plotted together to come and fight against Jerusalem and stir up trouble against it" (Nehemiah 4:8). Opposition came in accusations and lies. One opposer, Sanballat, accused Nehemiah and his group that "you and the Jews are plotting to revolt" (Nehemiah 6:5–7). The opposition will do anything to keep you from being successful.

This is how our enemy works. He will question you. He will scare you. He will accuse you. He will deceive you. He will do anything possible to keep you from accomplishing your mission and purpose. That is because he is out to steal, kill, and destroy. Nehemiah did not let his detractors deter him. Nehemiah's eyes were focused on his hope that God would help him restore the Jerusalem walls. When he was questioned, his faith assured him that "the God of heaven will give us success" (Nehemiah 2:20). Nehemiah did not let fear keep him from the work. When threatened, he organized using his resources to address the concern (stationing families to keep watch for invasion or arming all the workers) while keeping his hand to the work (Nehemiah 4:13). When accused, he called out and exposed the false accusations made against him (Nehemiah 6:8). Opposition to your restoring will occur. Plan for it and guard against it.

Another issue that will arise with any big project is discouragement. It may come because of weariness or fatigue. It may come in the form of feeling doubt or losing sight of the goal. Whatever the reason or way, it is common to experience when the mountain is God-sized. When this ploy of the enemy happens, you must step back and see the bigger picture. You need to see the forest for the trees. Sometimes our vision can become so narrowed or focused that it is helpful to step back and see the whole thing to appreciate our part in it all. We need to be reminded of the grander scope. This is what Nehemiah did with the people. He reminded them of the faithfulness of our "great and awesome" Lord (Nehemiah 4:14). Have patience. All large projects take time and require patience.

Completing a huge project does wonders for a person. Experiencing big-project completions is so fulfilling. In Nehemiah 6:15, we are told that "the wall was completed ... in fifty-two days." Faith is bolstered by the moments in Nehemiah 6:15. It might be completing a large school project or achieving a goal at work. It might be watching something that was broken down, like Jerusalem walls, restored. Restoration of something you trusted God for reinforces the fact that "if God is for you, who can be against you?" (Romans 8:31). Do not shrink back from these opportunities. Like Nehemiah, follow your heart and seek out God's mission for you. Seek to serve Him with your work and efforts (Colossians 3:17).

PATIENCE IN THE WILDERNESS OF LIFE

Patience is a virtue. Patience can be hard but worth it. For Nehemiah, even though fifty-two days was a short time to build such an immense wall surrounding such a grand city, each day must have felt like a month. When you are faced with questions, threats, accusations, discouraged workers, doubt, and so much more, patience is easy to run short. Nehemiah gives us a good example to follow when scaling our own mountains.

My valley required plenty of patience when there was no timetable for movement in the many unknowns of life. I decided I had to make lemonade out of the self-cultivated lemons I was dealing with. I applied myself to work on those things I could control. I worked on becoming a better person. I would love to say it was met with immediate success, but being stretched and taught takes time. The future was going to be a lengthy task of unmaking myself and being remade. This would take patience.

There was a song that I programmed as my wake-up music each day. It was a good reminder for the start of every day. It was a song based on Psalm 130 called "I Will Wait for You." The version I used was performed by a group of two men named Shane, appropriately named Shane & Shane. The song is written by Keith Getty, Jordan Kauflin, Matt Merker, and Stuart Townsend:[41]

> So put Your hope in God alone.
> Take courage in His power to save.
> Completely and forever won
> by Christ emerging from the grave.
>
> I will wait for You, I will wait for You.
> On Your word I will rely.
> I will wait for You, surely wait for You
> 'Til my soul is satisfied.

Patience involves waiting. There is no one better to wait on than your Lord and Savior, Jesus. He is trustworthy, faithful, and worthy of placing your hope in. He is sovereign over all things. His timing is perfect. If you are in a season of waiting, be patient. Wait expectantly and have faith in God's leading.

PERSONAL QUESTIONS

1. How have you had to wait expectantly with patience in your life?

2. What benefit does having patience bring to your life?

3. What thoughts battle within your mind, and how do you overcome destructive thoughts?

4. How do you need patience in your life's mission and purpose?

5. How do you need to wait for the Lord?

6. What do you really want for your life?

Patience is vital when navigating the road of restoration.

Chapter 11
ALMOST TO THE BOTTOM

> We rejoice in our sufferings, knowing that suffering produces perseverance, and perseverance produces character, and character produces hope, and hope does not put us to shame.
>
> —Romans 5:3–5

PERSEVERANCE

Some who are reading this have been able to run 26.2 miles at one time (no shame if you walked even a little of it). That feat is impressive. People run it all the time. Especially Kate Jayden of the UK. I read about her as I was reading the news one day. On December 31, 2021, she began running the marathon miles daily. That workout became a daily routine that lasted for the next 106 days! She finally stopped on April 15, 2022. I guess she had to do her taxes at some point. Her fastest time of those 106 trips was on day twenty-one. She ran the 26.2 miles in three hours and thirty-four minutes. But there is more. An incredible fact within that stretch is that at some point, right around day forty-six, her knee started hurting. In May, she had an MRI done and discovered a fracture in her knee.[42]

Running a marathon requires many qualities. To achieve success in such an experience requires planning and training. To finish the race, it will take resilience, endurance, and perseverance. Do you know the difference among these three qualities? They are different from one another.

Resilience is the strength and ability to recover from misfortune. Along the way, you may encounter problems, such as rocky terrain, various physical pains, or mental breakdowns. Resilience will help you push forward. If there is one thing you can count on in life, it is that obstacles will show up in anything you face. Sometimes they can be anticipated and prepared for, but other times, obstacles can come with no warning. How will you respond? Your response will teach you a lot about yourself and how resilient you are.

Endurance is having the ability and stamina to handle difficult things; 26.2 miles is a long distance to travel on foot. This distance takes training over time to build up the muscle strength and agility required. Marathon runners begin months in advance to prepare their bodies. Kate Jayden did not decide on New Year's Eve morning to go for a lengthy jog only to run the distance of a marathon. Then, deciding she liked the distance, she ran it again for 105 more days straight. She had been preparing for it. To finish this long journey, it will require endurance to complete. Endurance overcomes difficulty.

> *Perseverance leads to stronger hope and character.*

Perseverance is being persistent despite the adversity we face. Perseverance forces us to become the person the situation requires us to be. Our lives experience the most growth in times of perseverance. Perseverance leads to stronger hope and character.

Perseverance is greater than endurance. Consider endurance as you move from point A to point B through the difficulty. By the time you get to point B, you are essentially a more tired version of yourself than you were at point A. Perseverance is different. By the time you get to point B, you are not the same person that you started at point A. You must change to overcome the adversity you face along the way. Perseverance grows your character and resolve in greater ways so that you have been forever changed by the experience.

In a wonderful article by Brandon Young entitled "Perseverance Is Greater than Endurance: 5 Factors of Perseverance in Adversity," he outlines the differences between perseverance and endurance based on lessons he learned while being deployed in Afghanistan in the military.[43]

1. Perseverance involves change without control. With endurance, the difficult things you encounter are generally predictable and can be prepared for. Perseverance often means trudging through unexpected and uncontrolled realities.
2. Perseverance involves uncertainty. When enduring, you may be shaken, but you can still be confident. You can generally be sure you will make it through. When persevering, your confidence is shaken while you push through. There is a level of uncertainty that you will make it through.
3. Perseverance involves deeper choices. Endurance requires skills-based solutions. You perform the skills you have been taught to overcome the difficulty. Perseverance requires character-based solutions. You choose to live what you believe to help overcome adversity.
4. Perseverance involves acceptance. With endurance, you plan for the expected and have no sense or concern for the unknown. In perseverance, you have a sense of concern for the unknown. You must hope for the best but prepare for the worst. You do not have to like it, but you must accept it. You must accept the consequences, embrace the unpredictability of the situation, and expect more adversity.
5. Perseverance involves growth. It changes us. The fire of perseverance will refine you, and you will be better for it. It may take you time and reflection to recognize the growth.

Life is hard. On any given day, what is thrown at you is difficult and demanding. Adversities and obstacles are an unpleasant fact. No one has been promised an easy path. Your response in these situations will shape who you become. Will you just endure, pretending it is just difficult, and use the same plan, same approach, and same perspective that leads to the same diminishing results? Or will you recognize adversity for what it is and push to persevere, embracing growth along the way? Embracing perseverance is life-changing. Years down the road, when people ask how you did it, you will be able to answer like Brandon, "I persevered because I had to but grew because I chose to."

Those who follow Jesus have an incredible gift given to them that can make perseverance easier. The gift is the promised Holy Spirit, who lives within the believer. He is called our helper and our advocate. He is the believer's guide and instructor in adversity. He has promised never to leave us and is always there when called upon. The Holy Spirit is miles ahead of Google or YouTube in helping us address problems. The Holy Spirit comes at a cost, though. A cost that Jesus paid for us with His life.

Learn to call on the Holy Spirit, whether you are persevering or not. It is truly a life-giving thing to do. Your life will be transformed over time, and you will have help with situations requiring perseverance. He was my rock in the valley and the wilderness. In the months to come, dealing with judgment and consistent trials could have buried me in shame and guilt. However, I chose to persevere and let it change me. The Holy Spirit helped me keep my feet on the steady foundation of God's love and acceptance.

PURPOSEFUL PERSEVERING

I was now past a year into the valley, and progression was going painfully slow. It is common for things not to go at the speed we want them to, whether it be too slow or too fast. I wanted the legal hearings to proceed faster. The consequences, on the other hand, could wait. I was anxious to get the legal stuff done. Having the remaining hearings and the unknown future hanging over my head just added weight to my shoulders. I knew that I needed to keep my faith strong and push through the adversity I was facing. I needed to persevere.

It always helps to have something enjoyable ahead to fixate on. As you see it approaching, these anticipated moments help the time pass a little faster. They help you get through the mundane moments of life.

This is like the person who has a vacation coming two months from now. They have been planning and preparing; and before you know it, the time has passed, and it is time to go! This is like a high school senior whose graduation day is just over three months away. The countdown is well underway, and tasting that freedom is motivational every day.

Now, if just being patient for that day to come is what it entails, then you just need endurance to deal with the difficulty of waiting. What if you add adversity to the mix? Maybe that high school senior had issues with passing grades. The "senior slide" had caught on a little too early, and they were facing the need to improve quickly. The requirements of studying, retaking tests, and getting extra credit work in lieu of being out having fun were creating the need to persevere. That is what adversity gives us: opportunity for growth and improvement.

When you need to persevere, the need to pass on fun things is common. For me, knowing the adversity I was facing was self-induced meant not being able to attend occasions with my family. I could not vacation or celebrate holidays and birthdays and other occasions because of restrictions. This would often make me sad, and I would wonder if there was anything to look ahead to with anticipation. I was intentional about keeping myself busy and productive, which helped. However, looming ahead was the dark cloud of plea and sentencing.

This was a challenging time that led to personal growth from the adversity in my life. That is what perseverance will do: growth. I am aware the amount I had to persevere was not as severe as many other people. However, regardless of the severity of the adversity, there is a fact that remains true. Your mindset is critically important. I have kept in mind that when it feels like life is handing me lemons, there is always someone who has it worse than I do. I *will* get through this. Perseverance requires a positive mindset. Perseverance keeps the focus on the possibility, not the obstacle.

The dates for plea and sentencing finally arrived. The plea was one date, and sentencing was scheduled for one month later. I had never been in a courtroom before and will not plan on ever going back. Receiving news of your freedom being taken away brought many varying emotions. I was told that I was going to spend some time in jail. I had one month to arrange for life to progress in my absence. I had heard stories of what it would be like, so I prepared mentally for that. I wrote and prepared letters to be mailed to myself that would give encouragement during my stay. Productivity is a helpful way to persevere.

Adversity knows no limits. You might think that a situation could not get worse and that it may be over, but then you find out it is not. Two weeks after the sentence was given, I was notified that a meeting had been set up with a member of human resources at my job. I also noticed that my boss will be in attendance. I immediately saw the writing on the wall, and I was right in my presumption. The new "label" that came with the sentence prevented me from being able to work there anymore. A detail in my sentence allowed me to be released each workday to go to my job. After that meeting, that privilege was gone.

The apostle Paul knew many moments that required perseverance. In his ministry, he saw constant conflict and the adversity that came with introducing new teaching to Gentile peoples. Paul was God's chosen apostle to bring Jesus's teaching to the non-Jews. This was not an easy task by any means. It led him to be stoned, flogged, beaten, imprisoned, and ultimately martyred. Still, through all that, he wrote some of the most incredible books found in the New Testament of the Bible. One of those is the letter to the Romans. In Romans 5:3–5, Paul speaks on the purpose of perseverance. These verses helped me when I was in the valley. He says,

> We also glory in our sufferings, because we know that suffering produces perseverance, perseverance, character; and character, hope. And hope does not put us to shame, because God's love has been poured out into our hearts through the Holy Spirit.

God is always in control, even if it seems otherwise. There is a purpose in every hardship. Perseverance will grow your character and give you hope if you embrace it. Your restoration just may be dependent on it.

MURDERER MOSES

Moses knew many instances of life going wrong and the future looking bleak. The book of Exodus begins with an order that was placed for all Jewish newborns to be thrown into the Nile River and drowned. The king of Egypt was becoming afraid that the Hebrew nation was growing too big. So when Moses was born (Exodus 2), he was hidden as long as possible from the authorities (three months). Eventually, it was clear that something had to be done. He was put into a basket coated with tar and pitch and hid among the reeds along the Nile conveniently close to where Pharaoh's daughter went bathing. As the story goes, he was found, adopted, and grew up in the Pharaoh's household.

In Exodus 2:11, after Moses grew up, he came out to where the Hebrews were working and watched them at their hard labor. A part of him still identified with his people, and when he saw an Egyptian beating on a Hebrew, he acted. Verse 12 says, "Looking this way and that and seeing no one, he killed the Egyptian and hid him in the sand." He took out his rage on the Egyptian, resulting in murder. Then Moses gave him a sandy grave. He thought it was all done in secret and that no one knew. Until the next day. "The next day he went out and saw two Hebrews fighting. He asked the one in the wrong, 'Why are you hitting your fellow Hebrew?' The man said, 'Who made you ruler and judge over us? Are you thinking of killing me as you killed the Egyptian?'" (Exodus 2:13–14). Moses realized that they knew. His murderous background was exposed. What next? Well, next is that Pharaoh found out and put a death price on Moses's head. So Moses fled. He left fast.

Running from your problems is common. Who wants to face their issues? It is easier to ignore them if you can. The problem is that your problems will eventually catch up with you. Moses did not face his real problem, and it followed him. What was his problem? Moses's problem was that he was not living true to his real identity. After forty years of living the good life in Pharaoh's house, a part of him identified with Pharaoh. However, because he knew he was a Hebrew by blood, a part of him also identified with his people—that is, God's people, the Hebrews.

Certainly, this was behind his murder of the Egyptian. But now, his people were afraid of him, and this identity problem had him on the run.

Moses ran away to Midian. This was a long distance from Egypt. It was not a city but a land on the eastern side of the Sinai Peninsula bordering both sides of the Red Sea. Midian was the area where Israelites would one day wander in the wilderness after their miraculous Red Sea passage. As Moses was fleeing for his life, he thought that his future was marred, and he was now disqualified from being useful. Surely, Moses saw himself somewhat as a leader of his people with his palace background and grooming. But now what? Obviously, the Hebrews did not all see him with that same view. Now, there was nothing he could do. The interesting thing is when a person reaches that point, that's usually right where God likes us. That is when we finally get moldable, like clay to the potter.

Moses would spend the next forty years in Midian. During this time, Moses got married to Zipporah and had a son named Gershom. Life goes on after our failures. All the while, God is grooming us for His purposes. Moses did not realize this, but while he was away from Egypt, God was preparing the scene. The Hebrews were being worked harder and harder, and their prayers were being heard. God was preparing Moses for His purposes. You are never too far gone to be used by God. God just might be preparing the scene. It is all done in His time, and that time is perfect.

One day, Moses was tending the flock when he happened upon a bush engulfed in flames but was not being burned up. Moses thought, "I will go over and see this strange sight" (Exodus 3:3). When he got to the bush, the Lord called to him from within the bush, saying, "Moses, take off your sandals, for the place where you are standing is holy ground." From the bush, the Lord laid out his plans for Moses. The Lord had heard the cries of His people, and He was concerned for their suffering. He had plans for Moses to return to Egypt and to lead the people out of Pharaoh's rule. Moses was back in the game.

So, of course, Moses was hyped up and ready to go (sarcasm). No, not quite. Moses still had his unresolved identity issue. Thus began a series of identity-issue-revealing questions. They came and went like this:

1. "Who am I that I should go to Pharaoh?" (Exodus 3:11). God's answer was "I will be with you and here is the sign that I have sent you, you will worship on this mountain with my people" (Exodus 3:12).
2. "What if I go and they question who sent me?" (Exodus 3:13). God's answer was "Tell them 'I Am who I Am' has sent you" (Exodus 3:14). Then the plan was spelled out further for Moses.
3. Again, he questioned the Lord, "What if they do not believe me?" (Exodus 4:1). God's answer to Moses was "Watch what I can do through you." He made his staff become a snake and changed his hand from clean to leprous and back to clean. "I will do miracles through you."
4. "I have never been eloquent in speech" (Exodus 4:10). God's answer was in the form of questions. "Who gave you your mouth? Who helps you speak? I do. Trust me. I will help you and teach you" (Exodus 4:11).
5. "Please send someone else" (Exodus 4:13). God, though angry now, listened and had compassion. He offered his brother Aaron to go with him to help.

God is okay with our questions. But in your questions, do not doubt your identity. You were created for a purpose. Sometimes it takes time to learn what that is, but do not doubt that you have a purpose. Part of persevering is learning about that purpose. There is an identity-giving, restoring God who has purposes for you (Jeremiah 29:11). Trust Him. Moses did. He trusted God, and the rest of the story is miraculous. He returned to Egypt and led the Israelites out of Egypt. Through perseverance, the Israelites' freedom was restored, their identity as God's chosen people was restored, and Moses's identity after failure was restored.

IDENTITY MATTERS

The world around us likes to label people. They would look at Moses as a murderer. That title would dog him and label him for the rest of his life. God sees it differently for the person who has placed faith in his Son, Jesus. That person is labeled "forgiven." Those who trust Jesus's death and resurrection to save them from their rebellion against God are forgiven. We must choose to see ourselves as God sees us, not as the world does. This is a paradigm shift in our heads. It is a difference maker for our identity. When you choose to align your faith differently, your ability to persevere in life changes. Your path of perseverance leads you to a place of being spiritually purposed. That is a beautiful place to be.

Ben Fuller wrote and recorded a song that speaks of a person's identity.[44] It was influential to me when I began to listen to opposing voices in my life. Voices that would try to remind me of my past and who I must be inside.

> Who I am in the eyes of the Father
> Who I am His love set free
> Who I was I left at the altar
> I am Yours Lord, I believe.
> It's who I am.
> I'm a child of the most-high God and the most-high God's for me

My sentence gave me a title, a label, but it is not who I am. I refuse to be identified in that way. Perhaps there are some who would treat me differently because of it, but it isn't who I am. I have chosen a greater label: forgiven child of God. Identity is huge. Your identity matters! Choose to see yourself through the lens that Jesus sees you, and you will experience a life that is much more vibrant and freeing.

PERSONAL QUESTIONS

1. In what instances have you had to endure or persevere in life?

2. How has perseverance grown you into a better person?

3. How might you be fighting an identity problem in your life?

4. Where do you find your identity?

Perseverance leads to stronger hope and character.

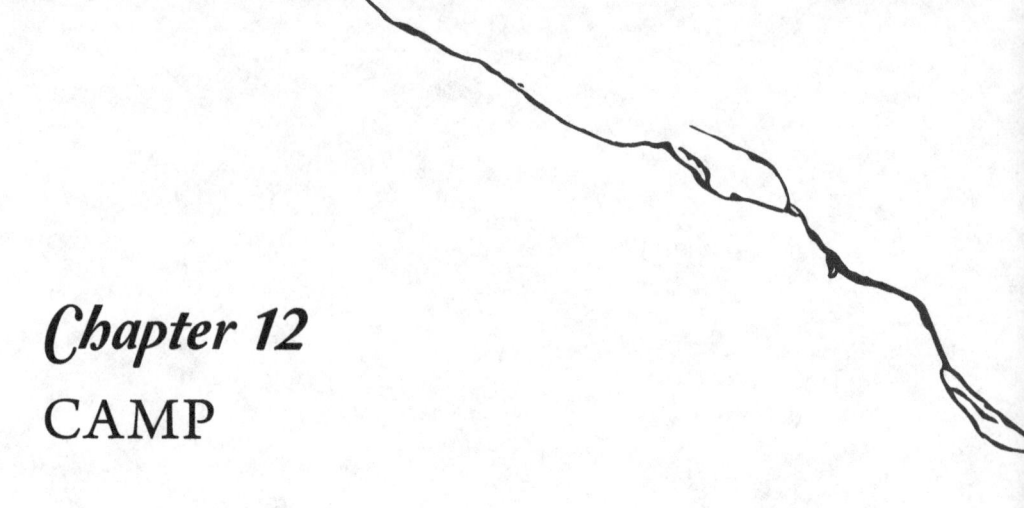

Chapter 12
CAMP

> Therefore, I urge you, brothers, in view of God's mercy, to offer your bodies as living sacrifices, holy and pleasing to God—this is your spiritual act of worship.
> —Romans 12:1

WORSHIP

On December 17, 2022, the Indianapolis Colts played an NFL game against the Minnesota Vikings. The Vikings came into the game as the favorites, having a far better record and playing at home. The game began, and surprisingly, it was dominated by Indianapolis. It was an embarrassment of mistakes that led to the Colts ahead at halftime by the score of 33–0. What transpired in the second half of the game nobody could have foreseen. Minnesota fans certainly knew their team had an electrifying offense and no doubt expected to see their team come out and perform better. However, they did not so much foresee them coming back to win the game 39–36. It was the largest comeback in the history of the NFL. It was an incredible game!

Stephen M. Newman describes nine different expressions that we use to worship.[45] The nine methods are the following:

1. Speaking
2. Shouting

3. Singing
4. Bowing
5. Standing
6. Dancing
7. Playing instruments
8. Clapping
9. Lifting hands

Every one of these was on display repeatedly during that record-setting football game. Now, to be clear, it is possible to celebrate something without worshipping it. But it is all too easy to involve worship in the things that excite us repeatedly. It is common and natural to celebrate the things that "fill our cup" and satisfy us, even if it is temporal.

Worship is many things:

1. An expression—Worship expresses reverence and adoration toward something or someone.
2. A noun—It is a posture of praise and adoration.
3. A verb—It is the action of ascribing worth and value.
4. A behavior—It is a behavior of devotion that leads the worshipper to submit their lives and desires in support of the worshipped. It is who we become. I am a huge Pittsburgh Steelers fan and have been known to slide into the practice of "worshipping" the black and gold during the fall. (I have repented.)

We are all worshippers. You cannot get around it. It is natural for humans to worship. It is how we are wired. It is what we are purposed to do (Romans 14:11). The question to ask is "What or who do you worship?" Pay attention to the first thing that comes to mind after reading that question. What is it? Write it down. Now, think even deeper about it. Is this a programmed answer? Is what I think I worship really what I worship? How does your life demonstrate that answer? Do your finances show that you are sold out to it? Does the way you spend your time reflect your devotion to it? Too often, worship is done subconsciously in our lives, and it is easy to be unaware of it.

Humankind is prone to worshipping different things. We worship what makes us feel most fulfilled. We worship those things that excite us and consume us. The object(s) of our worship may be sports, concerts, or some other entertainment source. That object may be our job. This is common because we invest so much of ourselves in what we do and work hard at it. It can easily become our identity. The object may be another person because of how they treat you. It may be sex, drugs, or music.

There is a major flaw in worshipping these types of things. It is all self-focused. It depends on what they do for you and how they make you feel. Worship is not self-seeking. Worship must be outward focused. If that job is lost, what would that do to you? If that person left, how would that affect you? When that team loses, how does your passion for them change?

> There is only one worthy of worship. His name is Jesus.
> All other things, in time, will fail you.

Read those three sentences again and engrave them in your heart. They are the truth. One other thing about worship is it is a command. The Bible commands us to worship (Psalm 96:9, 100:2; John 4:24, among others). This command is specific in that worship is only to be of the Lord. Only Jesus is worthy of our worship. What He has done for us will never be undone. Jesus loved us so much, and it shows because of the suffering He endured on the cross. He is worthy because His resurrection wiped away the penalty (spiritual death) for our sins that we should have had to pay. And because of that, we are gifted with the chance to spend eternity with Him, the very one we rebel against, if we would receive Him as our Savior and embrace His forgiveness (John 3:16). He alone is worthy of our worship.

Our God is a jealous God (Joshua 24:19)—jealous of our worship put toward other things. He has promised to never leave us or forsake us (Deuteronomy 31:8). He is faithful to us (1 Corinthians 1:9). He has forgiven us and offered us grace (Ephesians 2:8). His love for us is greater than we can understand (Isaiah 40:28).

Worship changes you. It is an act of honor that brings about a spirit of obedience toward the object you worship. Think about it, you worship what you chase after. You want more of it because you understand how good it is. Psalm 34:8 says, "Taste and see that the LORD is good; blessed is the one who takes refuge in him." When you have truly tasted and experienced the goodness of God, it changes how (and what) you worship.

Worship is also a response. It is acknowledging the work of God in your life. Understanding that God is good should lead you to a response of worship. One such response involves sacrifice: your will for the will of God. It is the laying down of your desires and seeking out and embracing the desires of God. For some, this is an arduous process because we like our sins. I can tell you from experience that there is nothing greater than living aligned with God's desires for your life. Our desires and dreams pale in comparison to what God has for us.

There is nothing that will change your life quicker than learning to worship Jesus. Worship resizes your perspective and cleans the lens through which you see life. It takes the focus off you and tunes you in with your Creator. Worshipping Jesus gives you the strength to carry on in difficult circumstances. It is like supercharged, high-octane fuel to rev us up when trials flare. It was vital for me in the valley and when I went to "camp."

> *Worship resizes your perspective and cleans the lens through which you see life.*

CAMP

One of the most humbling moments came when a judge told me that I would spend time in jail. This was hard for me to accept. Maybe it was pride that made it so hard. Maybe it was shame and embarrassment. I just did not like saying it. So I did not. Instead, I decided to put a spin on it and started calling it camp. I decided to treat it like I was going to summer camp.

I did not have much knowledge of what to expect. I talked to several people who had told me some things to expect. My mother loves to watch crime dramas on TV, so some of my perceptions came from that. Do not believe everything you see on TV. I wrote myself letters, stamped and addressed them, and gave them to my wife to send to me at regular intervals. I sent myself song lyrics, fun things to read, encouraging notes, and study questions from a group I was in. I could not bring anything in with me, so that was the method of delivering stuff for me to do.

The first night was the roughest of my life. I reported and then spent two hours in a room with nothing to do. I prayed and worshipped Jesus. After a while, a few guards came out and started checking us in. They took us back, and we got changed into our orange. Then, it was to another room to wait for another four hours with nothing to do. I prayed and worshipped God. Finally, at 2:00 a.m., they took me to my "room." I lay down on the mat on the concrete bed, and the dam broke. All the emotion of being at camp finally had an opportunity to surface, and the tears gushed out. It was humbling and scary. It was beyond lonely, as if I were abandoned on a deserted island. There was a spiritual heaviness in that place and time, and I just cried out to God for comfort. Eventually, exhaustion won over, and I was able to sleep.

There were two things that helped the days pass by quickly. The first was establishing a routine, and the second was being productive. I saw a lot of people sitting around and playing cards or watching movies all day long. I certainly did some of that as well, but I wanted more. I wanted to make the most of the time I had. This was like a sabbatical from life, and I was not going to waste it.

Establishing a routine made time pass quickly. I knew the schedule of when I had to be locked in and when I could be in the day area. I planned my days to accomplish what I wanted in the most efficient way.

Productivity made the time pass the quickest, and I felt good about my use of time. I set some goals for myself to achieve while I was camping. During my time there, I read fourteen books, read the Bible 1.5 times, wrote twenty-five letters, completed five homework assignments for a group I was in, and finished a whole book of crossword puzzles. I did regular exercise and walked the day area constantly.

I kept a Bible study going each night. One night, as I was walking, I was invited to join this group for a Bible study. I joined them, and we worshipped together. It was great! Within a week, three of the five guys were gone, and it was down to another man and me. Having led Bible studies in the past, I naturally took a leadership role to keep it going. It was just the two of us for a few days until some new men came to our pod. Then, we gained a few more. At the height of it, we had fourteen guys. We would open the Bible, read a passage, and talk about it. We would pray together afterward. It was very fulfilling and what I looked forward to every night.

The most impactful time would come as I would listen to the radio I had purchased. I enjoyed walking the day area and listening to Christian radio. I would lie in my bunk at night and listen to the music that led me. Each song was God focused and worshipful. I would experience a mental escape from my surroundings as I focused on praising Jesus. I loved and worshipped God, and this led to a strong connection with Him. Worship involves the passions of the heart, and it filled my cup to overflowing. Worship was crucial to keeping my heart and head in the right place. Jesus was my jailhouse "rock."

PETER AND PAUL IN PRISON

The early followers of Jesus tasted prison walls on several occasions. The message they were preaching was considered false testimony against many practices of the religious leaders, and prison was a temporary means of quieting them. Other times, exercising the power given to them by the Holy Spirit would cause uproar, and prison was their landing place while it was sorted out. Two such moments can be found in Acts 12:1–12 and 16:16–40. In each story, worship was the precursor to seeing a miracle happen.

The early church went through much persecution. There were many attempts to silence this group preaching about Jesus. King Herod saw that persecuting these early Christians was pleasing to many Jews, so he had Peter seized (Acts 12:3) since he was a leader of the group. He was going to have Peter brought to trial but needed to wait until after the Passover. All the while, "the church was praying to God for him" (Acts 12:4).

The night before the trial, a supernatural event took place. While the church was praying for him, "suddenly an angel of the Lord appeared, and a light shone in the cell. He struck Peter on the side and woke him up. 'Get up!' he said, and the chains fell off Peter's wrists" (Acts 12:7). The angel led Peter out past the first and second guards and through the iron gate leading to the city. He was not seen or stopped by anyone. Once he was a block away, the angel left, and Peter was free. A critical ingredient in this restoration to freedom was prayer and worship!

Another time, Paul and Silas were on the way to a place of prayer when a demon-possessed woman began harassing them. This went on for several days until Paul finally had enough of this annoyance (Acts 16:18). Turning to the woman, he cast out the spirit by the name of Jesus. The influence of this demon spirit was the source of their income, and so they brought them to the authorities with accusations against them. The crowd in the city joined in the accusations (Acts 16:22). As a result, they were stripped, beaten, flogged, and thrown in prison.

Most people in this position would be angry. They would surely cry out against the injustice of their imprisonment. That was not what Paul and Silas did. Their response was different. It is not to say that they were not feeling anger or resentment. They just chose to respond differently to their circumstances. They turned to worship. "About midnight, Paul and Silas were praying and singing hymns to God, and the other prisoners were listening to them" (Acts 16:25). What an example they were to the other inmates. The example they set was earthshaking—literally!

"Suddenly there was such a violent earthquake that the foundations of the prison were shaken. At once all the prison doors flew open and everyone's chains came loose" (Acts 16:26). The jailer thought they had all escaped, and he was ready to take his life. Letting prisoners escape would have meant death from his superiors, so he reckoned he might as well do it himself. Except that no one had escaped. Paul shouted out to the jailer that they were all still there. This story of restored freedom sees the jailer and his family come to saving faith in Jesus and are baptized—spiritual freedom granted. Paul and Silas are given physical freedom by the magistrates and officers. The critical ingredient in this restoration was worship!

WORSHIP MOVES GOD

Worship of God is the very means that can give us freedom! It was instrumental in giving Paul, Silas, and Peter their freedom. It is instrumental in giving all believers their freedom, both physically but, more so, spiritually. Worship takes our eyes off ourselves and our limitations and places hope and trust in God, who is able to do more than we could ever hope to do. He can move mountain-sized problems to grant us restoration.

My stint in jail was impactful. Establishing a routine and staying productive helped the time pass. Involving worship made it a time of growth and purpose. I have no desire to ever return to camp but will appreciate the time and the lessons learned while away. Everyone should take a purposeful sabbatical from life.

There are many worship songs that I enjoy. The songs that resonate most with me have lyrics that are directed straight at the Lord. These are prayer songs. Matt Maher, Daniel Carson, Jesse Reeves, Kristian Paul Stanfill, and Christy L. Nockels together wrote a prayer song that illustrates our most basic need.[46] The song is called "Lord, I Need You."

> Lord, I come, I confess
> Bowing here, I find my rest
> Without You, I fall apart
> You're the one that guides my heart.
> Lord, I need You, oh, I need You
> Every hour, I need You
> My one defense, my righteousness
> Oh God, how I need You.

I pray that your heart will be moved to embrace the lyrics of this song and to cry out to Jesus to be your Savior. Everything you need in life can be found in Him. Jesus delights to bless His followers. All it takes is a prayer admitting your sinfulness, a pledge to turn from it, and a desire to let Jesus be the Savior of your life.

PERSONAL QUESTIONS

1. What is the object of worship in your life? What evidence in your life leads to this answer?

2. In what ways do you worship throughout the day?

3. How does worship influence your perspective?

4. What is keeping you imprisoned in your life, and how do you need freedom?

Worship resizes your perspective and cleans the lens through which you see life.

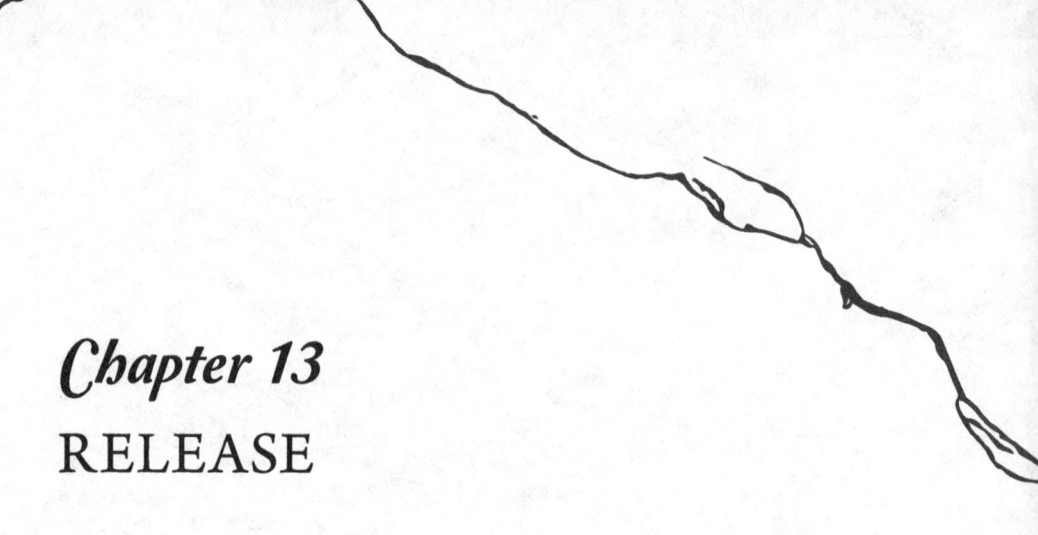

Chapter 13
RELEASE

> Now the Lord is the Spirit, and where the Spirit of the Lord is, there is freedom.
> —2 Corinthians 3:17

FREEDOM

It was April 18, 1775, and the redcoats from Britain were setting off from Boston toward Concord, Massachusetts. Their plan was to seize weapons and ammunition that the American colonists had stockpiled there. Tension had been building between the American colonies and Britain. The British had been imposing greater control over the colonies by implementing greater taxation to help pay for their defense during the French and Indian War (1754–1763). The colonists' resistance led to this fateful day in American history. The British troops met up with about seventy minutemen (an organized and trained New England militia) in Lexington. On that day, a shot was fired, which began the fight that left eight colonists dead and many injured. It was the start of the Revolutionary War. During this war, the colonies would declare independence from Britain and secure its future through victory. Through this war, the United States won freedom.[47]

Freedom does not come without a price. Retired US Air Force colonel Walter Hitchcock is credited with saying, "Freedom is not free."[48] During the Revolutionary War, an estimated 6,800 Americans were killed in action. An estimated seventeen thousand additional deaths occurred resulting from disease and death while prisoners of war. This was a heavy price to pay for freedom. Since that time, there have been many more wars and battles fought for the purpose of freedom. Many lives have been lost to protect this right. Each year, on the final Monday of May, we remember those who have died protecting our freedom. It is arguably the most underrated holiday celebrated in the United States. We call it Memorial Day.

I heard it asked, "What does freedom mean for you?" The answers were varied. Some of the answers were the ability to love, peace of mind, options, money, ease, breathing, and home. In some ways, many of these ideas involve living without bondage. Bondage involves the state of being restrained by or subjected to a controlling force. Freedom is living without bondage. Prior to the Revolutionary War, the American colonists were in bondage to British rule. During the American Civil War (1861–1865), a major tension surrounded the ownership of slaves. As a result of this costly war, freedom was won for slaves who had been in bondage. Virtually all wars and battles are fought from one side for the purpose of being released from bondage and gaining or defending freedom.

All people are born into bondage because of our sinful nature. At the root, this bondage is the same for everyone. However, it manifests itself through different struggles for all people. No one escapes it. It is the poison living inside every human being. I wrote about it in chapter 5. It is disobedience to God's commands. We are commanded to love God with all our hearts, souls, and minds (Matthew 22:36). But you may struggle with your heart, soul, and mind by loving money or things (you know what that *thing* may be for you) or someone more than God. Perhaps a love for God is not even on your radar. All you can think about is getting what you want. This is the human condition. Contrary to what you might think, this is not the freedom for which you were purposed. This "freedom" leaves you in bondage because you will never be satisfied with enough.

We are commanded to love one another as we love ourselves (Matthew 22:39). But then, you find yourself in rage at that person who cut you off on the road. You get incensed at the person who does not think like you do and voices their differing opinions. You were irate at your neighbor who is "ruining the neighborhood" because he has not cut his lawn or watered it for at least three weeks. Is there freedom in all this negative emotion? No, your ill feelings toward others keep you in bondage. This type of thing is happening all the time. Pay attention to your negative thoughts and ask yourself, what is really going on? Who is the one in bondage to their thoughts and struggling with freedom?

There is another day every year that we celebrate freedom. This day is celebrated on the first Sunday after the first full moon after the vernal equinox. It is better known as Easter. This holiday is not about bunnies and eggs. This holiday is about freedom from the bondage of sin. It is about a battle that was won over spiritual death. It is about a gift of grace and life that was given to the undeserving. It is about a sinless Savior, Jesus, who died a sacrificial death to grant freedom to all who would believe in Him (John 3:16). This is the way to freedom from bondage—by accepting Jesus as your Savior. To repent from, meaning to stop doing and turn away from, the wrong that you do and accept the forgiveness and better life that Jesus has taught us to live. It is an attitude that is less of self and more of God. That is the path to true freedom.

The reason this will lead to freedom is because it does not depend on you. You are not good enough to break from the sin that keeps you in bondage. You must rely on the grace that God gives because of Jesus's death and resurrection if you want to receive freedom from your sin. Without choosing Jesus, this sin will eternally separate you from God, which will result in spiritual death. Jesus won the war over sin on your behalf by resurrecting from death. Yes, you will still struggle with sin in this life, but your eternal spiritual future is life and not death if you have received Jesus as your Savior.

Freedom from the bondage of sin is eternally rewarding, but it is not free. It cost Jesus his life. It is prudent for every person to offer their life, meaning their self-serving thoughts and desires, and to align their life with Jesus.

RELEASED TO LIVE FREE

Living in bondage and then experiencing freedom changes your perspective. Living in true freedom in Christ changes the way you see and approach your days. It helps you appreciate life. It helps you be thankful for what you have been given or accomplished. Living in freedom builds gratitude toward others, whether they return it or not. It helps you be less offensive. Living in freedom leads you to a place of peace, even if there is conflict all around you. In the middle of the conflict, living in freedom helps you come to a more long-term "forest" outlook than just the "tree" problem in front of you. If you are not experiencing this type of freedom, consider if you are still living a life in bondage.

Freedom is not hard to appreciate, but choosing to be freed of bondage is the tough part. Sometimes it takes losing it all and hitting the bottom to get us to the point where we realize that we need help. When we come to the realization that we need help, we come to the place where we can know that Jesus came to set us free. He is the only way that points to a life of freedom. He is the truth. In John 8:31–32, Jesus says, "If you hold to my teaching, you are really my disciples. Then you will know the truth, and the truth will set you free."

I have known Jesus for most of my life, but my life and commitment got seriously refined when I was locked up. In that space, I had time to reflect on life. I had time to talk to God in prayer, which included questioning, getting mad at, and even arguing at times. It is okay. God can handle all that. He simply wants us to come to Him (Matthew 11:28, 1 Peter 5:7). During my time at camp, I had time to dig deep inward and get an honest handle on how I tick. It was a humble time.

On Sunday, January 22, 2023, I was released from jail. I have never been so grateful to breathe in the cold zero-degree Minnesota winter air and to see the white snow covering the earth. I have never been so happy to see the ones I love and to receive their love in return. I have never been so appreciative of going out to a restaurant and tasting the sugary goodness and calorically excessive experience of pancakes, eggs, and bacon. Such a far cry from what I had gotten accustomed to.

The first place I wanted to go to was church. I know that some people have had bad experiences at church before. It is not a perfect place, and it is filled with sin-filled people. But the church is about connecting with God and with a community of followers. It is not about what it can do for you. I wanted to worship my Lord and Savior, who helped me endure and grow. I wanted to sing His praises and thank my Lord among a community of believers. I wanted to hear a challenging but encouraging word to lead me to think more deeply about Jesus. As I did all this, I experienced freedom as I focused all I had on the goodness of God. This makes sense because of what Jesus said in John 8:36, "If the Son [Jesus] sets you free, you will be free indeed." Focusing your life on Jesus will free you.

Choosing to follow our culture will keep you in bondage. Advertising keeps telling us all the things that you do not have but "need." If you buy into that, you will never be satisfied. Media tells you how you should live and how you should think. If you try to follow that model, you will never be complete. There are many outside influences telling you how to think, what to believe, and how to behave. As a society, we are constantly living with fewer morals and values. It is just like the time of the judges, as mentioned in Judges 21:25, "Everyone did as they saw fit." When this is the norm, beware! There is no freedom in that.

As I moved forward after camp, the near future was still unknown. I was still separated from my family, had no job, and had no timeframe for advancement—but I did have peace. I had a drive to write this book, a passion given to me while confined. I was driven to complete the requirements to reunite with my family. I had such a desire to be a better parent, and I got to practice with my son, who was in the hospital dealing with his own restoration story. The life for a follower of Jesus is not necessarily easy. That has never been promised. But through the struggle, there is a Savior walking with us through the Holy Spirit. He gives peace in conflict, joy in affliction, patience in the waiting, and love in the loneliness. All that brings freedom to life.

PRODIGAL SON

Jesus tells the story of a son who desired the joys of freedom—at least freedom as he dreamed it. The story can be found in Luke 15:11–32. Many have called it the parable (a story with a moral point) of the prodigal son. *Prodigal* means spending wildly and recklessly. In this story, a son went to the father and asked for an advance on his share of his inheritance. After receiving it, the son left and lived "freely" in a prodigal way. I imagine that life was enjoyable and that he had many friends. That is what money can temporarily buy you—that is, until the money runs out.

When we live with all abandon, it is easy to ignore the potential disaster that could occur because it does not fit well with our desires. Louie Giglio paints a clear picture when he tells the story of his honeymoon. The image of the view from their lodging looked amazing until he realized upon arriving that a boat graveyard was conveniently cropped out of the resort's photograph. That is what we do to any thoughts of disaster to our freedom plans. That is what the prodigal son did. He was so focused on his freedom plans that did not involve a plan for disaster.

The story says in verse 14, "After he had spent everything, there was a severe famine in that whole country, and he began to be in need." Uh-oh! Now what? What do you do when there is no family, your "friends" have left, there is no money, and your stomach continually reminds you that there is no food? Freedom has failed, and you are in bondage—a bondage you put yourself in by your decisions.

In the story, the son chose his next steps wisely. The text says, "When he came to his senses" (Luke 15:17). Maybe it was because there were no other options. Maybe it took hitting the bottom to jar his focus off himself. Maybe it is the point for all who are looking to get out of bondage. He humbled himself. He stepped back and saw what was going on in the big picture. He realized how his choices did not lead him to freedom but to be a prisoner of his circumstances. He thought about how much better the slaves back home lived compared to him, and they were slaves! He knew his father could help.

So he made a new plan. He set off to go back to his father. He produced a speech where he would plead to be accepted as a servant. He would confess to having sinned against heaven and against his father. He would confess that he is not worthy of being called his son. This plan was selfless. This plan would lead to true freedom. And no one saw the outcome of the execution of this plan coming. It is what Jesus does for us, which is the point of the story.

It says, "While the son was still a long way off, his father saw him and was filled with compassion for him" (Luke 15:20). This tells me that the father was watching for him. He had not given up hope that his son, who had chosen poorly, would repent and return to life with the father. A life of true freedom. The father waited with anticipation. And when he saw his son, it says, "He ran to him." He did not wait and let his son bow to him. He took off, which, in that culture, was an undignified thing to do. This just did not happen. But when a father sees his lost son returning, who cares what others think? His son was lost and is now back. That is what God does to us when we come seeking Him. He runs to us.

When the father got to his son, he "threw his arms around him and kissed him." He called for his servants to put a ring on his finger and sandals on his feet to get the fattened calf and kill it. "Get it on the spit and cook that baby! We are going to have a party tonight!" That is what happened. The whole town threw a party and celebrated the return of the prodigal son.

This is what the heavens do when we decide to return to God the Father, seeking true freedom from the bondage of our bad past decisions. They throw a party. They celebrate the choice made to return from that which leads to death and turn to that which gives life. Is there any better reason to celebrate? In seeking freedom, the son found the restoration he needed. A restoration that God makes possible.

FREEDOM THROUGH GRACE

Freedom is made full through the powerful gift of grace! It may seem counterintuitive that submitting to someone else would give you freedom, but it is the truth. We submit to the government and thus are granted the rights that come with our freedom. It is so with God as well. It is the best choice that a person can make. Life is not meant to be lived in bondage. Christ came so that we could be set free (Luke 4:18). I have been a follower of Jesus for most of my life. But I knew I could do better and could experience greater freedom. There is a song titled "New Creation." It is written by Mac Powell, Jeff Pardo, and Hank Bentley, and it describes who you and I are in Christ.[49] When you receive His gift of saving grace, He gives you the ability to become a new creation!

> *Freedom is made full through the powerful gift of grace!*

It wasn't 'til I stumbled and made my mistakes
That I could know in my soul how amazing was grace.
You brought me blessings out of a tragedy
You turned my old song into a symphony
And with Your Spirit living inside of me
I'm a new creation, I'm a new creation.

PERSONAL QUESTIONS

1. What does freedom mean for you?

2. In what way are you living in bondage to something?

3. What do you need to do to humbly seek the Lord for freedom?

4. In what ways are you and the prodigal son similar?

Freedom is made full through the powerful gift of grace!

Chapter 14
THE GREATER RESTORATION

> For it is by grace you have been saved, through faith—
> and this is not from yourselves, it is the gift of God—not
> by works so that no one can boast.
> —Ephesians 2:8–9

GRACE

Thomas was just a dusty-brown-haired young, twelve-year-old boy when his life was turned upside down. On a dark, cloudy day, his father physically abused him. He had been at home while his mother and three older brothers had gone to the store. The whole experience happened quick. Thomas accidentally knocked over an important family heirloom and broke it. His father went into a rage and struck Thomas in the face. What he remembers most about his father was the terror in his father's voice afterward. Thomas was scared. He did not know what to think. He didn't know what to do. He had been warned by his father to lie about the cut on his face. He was not to tell anyone, and he didn't for a few weeks. However, the frequent nightmares and fear couldn't be explained to his comforting mother. Finally, Thomas spoke up. She was incensed.

What transpired over the next few months left Thomas even further shattered and broken. He felt shame for speaking up about his father. He had loved his father, and they had so many good memories prior to that moment. He wished it had never happened. His parents seemed to fight nonstop about everything. Ultimately, his mother and father divorced. They assured Thomas that he was not the cause. All he knew was that now his family life had been split. He has since seen his brothers grow up with anger, and it has affected them greatly as well. He blamed himself. He struggled with so many emotions and saw many different therapists. He didn't know what to do, think, say, or feel. He just wanted to be left alone, even though that was the toughest place to be.

Two weeks ago, Thomas heard his church pastor speak about forgiveness from Matthew 6:14–15, which says,

> For if you forgive other people when they sin against you, your heavenly Father will also forgive you. But if you do not forgive others their sins, your Father will not forgive your sins.

The pastor spoke of the freedom from bondage that forgiving someone can give. Thomas felt like the pastor was speaking directly to him. He felt trapped and wanted to be free. He thought about that freedom often in the days after. He needed to talk to someone about it. He asked his mother about the pastor's message. After discussions with his mother and his therapist, Thomas came to realize that unforgiveness toward his father was what kept him holding on to his pain. He needed to forgive. But how? Did his father deserve forgiveness? No. He did not. But that is where grace comes in. Grace is getting what you do not deserve. His father did not deserve forgiveness, but offering him grace would help Thomas release the pent-up pain inside. Thomas resolved to communicate with his father.

After he spoke to his mother and therapists about it, they agreed to let him write a letter to his father. In his letter, he expressed his anger and his pain. In the letter, Thomas also expressed that he had decided to forgive his father and to offer grace, even though he hadn't asked for it or deserved it. It was just being given. Of course, this did not mean that they were reconciled, and there would still be protection in place. However, Thomas felt a sense of release from his anxiety after sending the letter.

Thomas knew that forgiving would be the hardest thing he had ever done. However, he also knew that not forgiving would be the most harmful thing he could do to himself. It was a fork in the road on the journey to his restoration.

Grace is a powerful force. Grace is undeserved favor toward another person. Grace is generosity that can help a stranger in need. Grace has respect for another person, regardless of who they are or what they have done. Grace is an action that leads to change. It can mend relationships. It can put out fires between people or groups. Grace has compassion for other people. It is a quality that can keep a person humble. Grace is an energy that can release a person to freedom.

Grace is best understood when you come to realize that none of us deserves anything from another person. Yes, we should treat one another with respect, love, and courtesy but not because anyone deserves it. We treat one another that way because we have been commanded to do so (Matthew 5:44, 22:39). We need to be constant extenders of grace toward others. This is easier to do when you understand the ultimate grace that has been offered to each of us by God through His Son, Jesus.

At the center of each of us is a selfish heart. We were not created this way by God. It has been passed on to every generation since the first sin of Adam and Eve (Genesis 3:6–7). Jeremiah 17:9 tells us that our hearts are deceitful above all things. Our default is to fulfill our own desires first. If you step back and listen to your immediate thoughts when others ask something of you, you will often see this happen. I have seen this in my life. Someone asks me to help them, and my first thought is regarding my own plans. Do I want to help, or what will it cost me? I think about myself instead of seeing a chance to help another in need and extending grace.

The books of wisdom in the Bible (Psalms, Proverbs, Ecclesiastes, Job, Song of Songs) are filled with statements that reveal the condition of our hearts. Many verses start out with "Do not let your heart be ____" because our hearts are sinfully filled with the tendency to do these things. I'm talking about a heart drawn to evil (Psalm 141:4), an envious heart (Proverbs 23:17), a heart that lusts (Proverbs 6:25), a heart that rejoices over another's stumble (Proverbs 24:17), a heart that is hasty to speak (Ecclesiastes 5:2), and several others.

Grace is often contrary to the heart's initial desire. Grace looks like helping a friend out when they are overwhelmed with housework. Grace looks like the kindness of a parent toward their misbehaving child. Grace looks like helping a stranded stranger because of a dead car battery. Grace looks like watching kids for a single parent so they can have a break. Grace can also look like forgiving yourself for your own misdeeds toward yourself and others. Grace can take on many forms.

Offering grace to another can be difficult, especially if the other has offended you in the past. Extending grace to others is not only selflessness but also requires giving of yourself. When grace is given, it holds no grudges. You may still feel pain and trauma, but grace chooses to release the past hurts held against the offender. Offering grace to another person is an impactful element in restoration from brokenness.

Receiving grace can restore as well. Receiving grace from others helps free you from shame and guilt. When someone extends grace to you, it aids in forgiving yourself. It leads you to humility when you understand that you are being given something that you do not deserve. This is where we find Jesus's gift so incredible.

We are commanded to be perfect (Matthew 5:48). This is an impossible command when left to our own selves. You cannot be perfect. I cannot be perfect. Sin was downloaded into us upon conception. All of us have sinned and fallen short of the perfection God requires (Romans 3:23). The problem with sin is that it only leads to spiritual death (Romans 6:23). If left to us, we are all doomed to eternal separation from God. This is a place known as hell. This is bad news. The good news is that God knew of our spiritual deficit, and so He gracefully sent His Son, Jesus, to pay the penalty we should have to pay (John 3:16). We can be saved from our sins because of the grace of God. Ephesians 2:8–9 says, "For it is by grace you have been saved, through faith—and this is not from yourselves, it is the gift of God—not by works, so that no one can boast." Placing faith in the gracious gift of Jesus's death and resurrection to save you from your sin will lead you to the greatest restoration.

Every reader of this book has something they wish could be restored in their life. Maybe you are hoping to have a relationship with another person restored. Maybe it is a physical ailment or mental struggle that you desire to be healed. Maybe someone close to you is very sick or is dying, and you are praying for a miracle. Maybe it is meaningful employment that was lost, and you need it restored. Whatever it is, something is broken, and you desire for it to be restored. The reality is that the restoration you seek cannot be promised. In situations like these, I cling to Jeremiah 29:11, where God promises that He *has* plans to prosper us and not harm us. He *has* plans for hope and a future in our lives. I can find comfort in those words; however, I also realize that God's ways are not my ways. No, His ways are better. And His ways may not look like what I want. The reality is that relationships may not ever be restored. That ailment or struggle may not be healed. Loved ones may die. Work may not be found. We are not promised a restoration on this side of physical death. But God's gift of grace and forgiveness for our sins means that there is *a greater restoration* promised to us. Better than anything we could experience in our lives here on earth.

This greater restoration will be experienced by believers after their physical death. There will be a time when we will stand before God and need to account for the things we have done on earth. At that moment, no person will be able to stand on their own. The only answer to why we should spend eternity in God's kingdom is that we place faith in the gift of grace that Jesus offers to us when we choose to follow Him. No amount of "I did this for you" will suffice. Any kind of "work" will come up empty. Only the choice to receive grace from Jesus and the choice to follow Him will lead you to great restoration and a place for eternity in the kingdom of God.

BEAUTIFULLY REMADE

I am not the same person today as I was at the time of my offense. My eyes have been opened, and much healing has taken place. Looking back, I can see the changes that have led me to a healthier me. I have used the two-plus years since being separated from my family to work on being a healthier person. It takes time to change habits and thought patterns. Moving from brokenness to restoration utilizes the elements I have described in this book.

I live more by faith and truth and utilize guidance now. My relationship with Jesus has been constant in my life, but it has grown stronger during my time in the valley. I've never been consistent for long periods doing a personal devotional time every day, though I know this is an important habit. I have committed to starting my day with Bible reading and prayer. I want to give the "first fruits" of my day, the best of me, to my God. The benefit of doing this is the regulation of my thoughts and emotions that start my day off on a straight course. My time praying taps me into the Holy Spirit, who gives me guidance. It strengthens my faith and leads me to the truth.

I live with more understanding of the impact of sin and the guilt and shame that it produces. My sin led me to self-consumed thought patterns. I felt that I was entitled to respect and affirmation. It inflated my estimation of myself and what I was owed. Inside, the inner me didn't match the outer me that others saw. Externally, I was living a life appearing as one person but hid the inner turmoil raging inside. I was wearing a mask because of fears and insecurities. Now, I can see how being true to God alone produces the best version of you. Aligning your inner and outer self to reflect the truth leads you to be who you want to be. I can live honestly with myself, and this exposes and diffuses the ploys of the enemy.

I live more with discipline and hope. I used to devote time to things and thoughts that didn't serve me in productive ways. I wasted a lot of time and effort dwelling on thoughts and doing things that served no purpose toward being a healthy person. This is what the enemy wants us to do. As I began to take my thoughts captive and make them aligned with Jesus (2 Corinthians 10:5), I found more positivity and encouragement. As I rid myself of time-wasting activities and focused more on spending energy on life-infusing and goal-centered tasks, I became more fulfilled in what I did. I found more purpose in life. All this gave me hope for the future, come what may.

I live more with patience, perseverance, and worship. I was wired with the skills of management. Often, this led to anxiety and worry over things I had no control over. Time in the valley helped develop a greater sense of patience. I trusted in the Lord's timing. This patience led to perseverance (Romans 5:4), which has grown my character in a more Christlike way. It has led me to a more worshipful way of living. I make consistent efforts to infuse worship of God in everything I do.

I live with freedom and with more grace toward others. I didn't realize the bondage that my destructive thoughts kept on me. I did not realize how much of a grip they had on me. I had to learn to recognize when they were present and to call them out. I decided not to let the enemy have a voice anymore. I decided that I would not do negative self-talk anymore. I decided that I did not do gluttony anymore. I decided that my life was not my own and that the one who bought me at a price (Jesus) had ownership (1 Corinthians 6:19–20). These decisions led me to experience freedom. I could forgive myself and receive the grace that Jesus has offered to me.

I still slip from time to time and choose to not live according to my values. This is becoming less and less every day. However, I have tools to help me with recognition. I frequently remind myself who I am in Christ because the enemy likes to remind me of who I once was. I spend less time with depressing thoughts because the lens that I used to see life through has been cleaned. I have people who help keep me accountable. I am so grateful for them. Life has moved from broken to beautiful. I am being remade and useful by the restoring God.

The change in my life was not done on my own. I had help from many people in changing the destructive mental patterns in my life to healthier habits. We all need help to be better people. *Together* is a beautiful word. We need to be a team, helping one another. That is what the body of Christ should look like (Ephesians 4:12). I'd like to call out several people who were used by God in my life. This is not an exhaustive list as there are people who have played smaller roles at different periods through the valley. I am so thankful to God for all of you.

First and foremost, I praise my Savior and Lord Jesus, who has been my rock and refuge through it all. You are worthy of all my life. To God be the glory! Next, I am thankful for the love and support from my wife, Kara. She has been amazing. She has been used by God to be a voice of encouragement and commitment. In this together, Lovely! I thank my parents, Mike and Sandie, who have been supportive in countless ways. They both have given support by way of food, lodging, listening, and a list that would extend for pages. Thanks to my sister, Shelly, who has been supportive from day one, asking the simple question, "How are you doing?" Feeling like someone cares is priceless. Thanks to my counselors from Texas, Pat and John, who helped my wife and me get back on track in our marriage. You have been so helpful. Gary, Adam, and Chad, you three have been godsent friends, who have aided with listening ears and encouraging voices. Thank you.

In chapter 2, I referenced a challenge I was given to describe myself in one sentence. If I were to answer that challenge today, it would be this: Brian Goodwin is a broken-to-whole remade work of His Savior, Jesus.

JESUS'S DEATH AND RESURRECTION

The most powerful restoration story of the Bible is found in all four gospel books: Matthew, Mark, Luke, and John. It is the story of God turned man who came and became a sacrificial lamb to atone for the sins of humanity. It is the story that makes reconciliation with God the Father possible. It is a story of grace and forgiveness. It is a story of unconditional love that defeats the enemy, Satan, and the power of death. It is a restoration story that leads to a greater restoration story and eternal life for all who follow Jesus.

The story of the Savior becoming man is celebrated every December at Christmastime. We remember the gift that God gave us in Jesus by giving one another gifts. It is a beautiful time of year to share kindness, love, and goodwill with others. The holiday has been very materialized in our culture, but the heart of the holiday is in giving.

Jesus's life was all about communicating a message of repentance and that He was the way to eternal life and freedom from the bondage of sin. He taught about the coming kingdom, a new covenant, and instructions on how to live in unity. During His thirty-three-year life, He healed the sick and lame. He removed evil spirits. He upset the religious leaders by correcting their doctrines and claiming to be God. This new teaching was what landed Him in trouble and led to His death by crucifixion.

In the springtime, we remember Jesus's death and resurrection at Easter. *Easter* is an Old English name, which simply means the "east." For the Christians, the sun that rises in the east—bringing light, warmth, and hope—is a symbol of the rising Christ, who is the true light of the world.[50] I like to think of it as resurrection Sunday. It is the foundation for Christianity. Without the resurrection, there would be nothing to worship. Jesus would still be in the grave, and our future physical death would still mean eternal spiritual death and separation from God. When you understand that Jesus's resurrection is the very means by which we can truly experience life, then you understand why He is worthy to be worshipped and followed. Too many people miss this critical truth.

The agony that Jesus went through leading to his death is mind-blowing. It was absolutely the worst, cruel, drawn-out punishment a person could experience. When you realize that Jesus lived a sinless life but that He chose to endure the pain for you and for me, it should lead to a desire to worship Him. Talk about amazing grace! The first pain He experienced was abandonment. All His followers left Him. The next pain was verbal. Jesus was barraged with lies, with people mocking, insulting, and laughing at Him. Then came the physical blows. He was flogged and tortured with whips made with shards that would rip his skin off. By the end of this torture, He was barely recognizable. With bone and muscle exposed, the pain had to have been excruciating. But then, they expected Jesus to carry the *stauros*, or horizontal crossbeam of His cross, up the hill to Golgotha, where He would be executed. He couldn't make it. He collapsed and needed help. Simon of Cyrene was ordered to help (John 19:17, Luke 23:26).

The last section of Jesus's crucifixion was being nailed to the cross and placed on the ground. With the strain on His lungs, the loss of blood, His nerves screaming in pain as thorns pierced his scalp, and nails that ran through his wrists and ankles, there is nothing more incredible a person could go through simply out of love for another. Jesus came to take the punishment we have earned for our disobedient sin. There is no bigger picture of grace than what Jesus endured on the cross for humanity. He is worthy of being praised.

After His death, His body was prepared and buried. The religious leaders remembered Jesus's words that after three days, He would rise. He was so revered and feared that guards were stationed outside the tomb to make sure no one tried to steal His body (Matthew 27:64). A big stone was rolled in front of the tomb and secured with a seal. I could imagine God the Father looking down, chuckling at these human efforts to keep Jesus's body entombed. Nice try, boys.

That was the first day in the tomb. The second day had to have been the longest day for Jesus's followers. I wonder what they were thinking. Jesus had told them He would rise. Did they forget, or were they anticipating it? I don't believe so because they were shocked upon hearing of the empty tomb the next day. Were they crushed in spirit, questioning, "Now what?" I imagine a very dark, dreary day, living in gloom and confusion. The Bible doesn't say.

I can think of times in my life when I felt like what I imagined the disciples felt like. The unknown brings you to that place. Having your eyes fixated on the present situation and not seeing hope brings you to that place. Stuck in your own life's muck and mire brings you to that place. But what happens when you gaze ahead to the third day? How is your spirit lifted when you fix your eyes on the victory that was won through Jesus's resurrection? That is where we find hope in our lives. Jesus was broken and was restored. We are broken, and we can also be restored because of the grace of Jesus. Your brokenness can be a beautiful restoration story.

The morning of the third day, the two Marys were taking spices to the tomb when they discovered the stone rolled away. Jesus was not there. He had risen from death. In the coming days, Jesus would appear before hundreds of people in a newly restored body. The gospel of Luke tells a story of Jesus walking along with two men on the way to Emmaus, talking about what happened concerning Jesus. They didn't know who they were with. He told them all about what the prophets had said concerning Himself, and they were amazed. He had dinner with them, wherein they realized His identity (Luke 24:13–35). Could you imagine meeting a random person at a store and hearing them talk in-depth about world events? Listening to them made things clearer and helped you understand to a greater extent. Then, later, you learn that it was the president of the United States (POTUS).

Jesus's resurrection is the most unbelievably good news. What do you think about someone dying and then coming back to life? People are skeptical about Jesus's resurrection. Even the disciples at the time had their doubts. We live two thousand years later, and people still question this event. There is evidence for the resurrection. Lee Strobel has a great book called *The Case for Christ*, which details his research into the proof of Jesus's resurrection.

During Jesus's trial, Pontius Pilate asked a pivotal question. In Matthew 27:22, Pilate asked, "What shall I do, then, with Jesus who is called the Messiah?" This is a question every person must answer. What are you going to do with Jesus? Reject Him? Ignore Him? Accept Him? Follow Him? What significance will you allow Him to have in your life? He has given us an amazing gift. The grace He offers leads to the greatest restoration. The request made by God to each of us is to turn from our wicked ways, receive his forgiveness and grace, and choose to follow Him by obeying His commands with our whole hearts, souls, and minds.

> *The grace Jesus offers leads to the greatest restoration.*

Elevation Worship recorded a song that describes the greater restoration from sin that believers will face in the future. It was written by Christopher Brown, Mack Brock, Matthew Thabo Ntele, Steven Furtick, and Wade Joye.[51] It is called "Resurrecting."

> Your name, Your name is victory
> All praise, will rise to Christ, our King.
> By Your Spirit I will rise
> From the ashes of defeat
> The resurrected King, is resurrecting me
> In Your name I come alive
> To declare Your victory
> The resurrected King, is resurrecting me

Regardless of what is happening in life—the brokenness you are experiencing, the pain you live with, and any unknowns lying in front of you—restoration is possible. Broken people do not need to stay broken. Have faith. Seek truth. Ask for guidance. Search your life for sin and deal with shame and guilt. Receive God's provision. Live disciplined. Find hope. Be patient. Persevere in life. Worship Jesus and experience freedom. Understand the grace of God and look forward to healing. You can be remade by the power of the restoring God.

PERSONAL QUESTIONS

1. What is your perception of grace?

2. Who do you need to extend grace to in your life? How will you show grace?

3. What parts of your life are destructive? How can you make changes to be more constructive?

4. Out of the thirteen elements discussed throughout this book, which one do you need a greater understanding to help you? Is it faith, truth, guidance, sin, guilt and shame, provision, discipline, hope, patience, perseverance, worship, freedom, or grace?

5. What keeps you from receiving Jesus as your Savior? If you have received His gift of grace, what needs to change to follow Him even closer?

The grace Jesus offers leads to the greatest restoration.

References

All scripture quotations, unless otherwise indicated, are taken from the NIV Study Bible, New International Version. Kenneth Barker, General Editor, Zondervan Bible Pub, 1984.

Scripture quotations marked (ESV) are taken from the English Standard Version of the Bible, e-Sword Bible App, version 13.0.0.

Introduction

1. Sho, Terushi. 2021. "Kintsugi: Japan's Ancient Art of Embracing Imperfection." Jan 8, 2021. https://www.bbc.com/travel/article/20210107-kintsugi-japans-ancient-art-of-embracing-imperfection.
2. Meyer, F. B. 1979. *F.B. Meyer Bible Commentary*. Tyndale House.

Chapter 1

3. Layton, Tasha. "Look What You've Done." Track 5 on *How Far*. BEC Recordings, 2022, CD.

Chapter 2

4. Regan, Sarah. 2021. "5 Common Traits of Middle Children + How to Use Them To Your Advantage." MindBodyGreen, 21 April, 2021. https://www.mindbodygreen.com/articles/middle-child-syndrome.
5. Jones, Alexis. 2018. "20 Things Only Middle Children Understand." *Woman's Day*, August 8, 2018. https://www.womansday.com/relationships/family-friends/g22663336/things-only-middle-children-understand.
6. Lights Worship. "Highs and Lows." Track 1 on *Highs and Lows*. Z Music, 2019, CD.

Chapter 3

7   Wikipedia contributors. 2023. "Truth." Wikipedia, October. https://en.wikipedia.org/wiki/Truth.
8   "Definition of Truth." 2023. In Merriam-Webster Dictionary. https://www.merriam-webster.com/dictionary/truth.
9   Pardi, Paul. 2015. "What Is Truth?" *Philosphynews.com,* 22 March, 2015. https://www.philosophynews.com/what-is-truth.
10 Blackburn, Simon W. 2022. "Truth." *Britannica.com,* 6 Oct. 2022. https://www.britannica.com/topic/truth-philosophy-and-logic
11 "Four Truths." n.d. https://www.hsdinstitute.org/resources/four-truths.html
12 Meyers, Rick. "Guzik's Commentary: John 14." e-Sword Bible app. Version 13.0.0.
13 Lerner, Max. 1959. *"The Unfinished Country: A Book of American Symbols."* Simon & Schuster.
14 McGee, Robert S. 2003. *"The Search for Significance."* Thomas Nelson.
15 Anderson, Neil T. 2020. *"Victory Over The Darkness."* Bethany House.
16 Crawford, Leanna. "Truth I'm Standing On." Track 1 on *Truth I'm Standing On.* Provident Label Group, 2020, CD.

Chapter 4

17 Meyers, Rick. "Judges 16:1-31." *Guzik's Commentary,* e-Sword Bible app. Version 13.0.0.
18 McGraw, Tim and Faith Hill. "Keep Your Eyes On Me." Track 2 on *The Shack: Music From and Inspired By the Original Motion Picture.* Atlantic Recording, 2017, CD.

Chapter 5

19 Crowder, David. "Forgiven." Track 8 on *American Prodigal.* sixstepsrecords/Sparrow Records, 2016, CD.

Chapter 6

20 Flinn, John. 2003. "Gory story of blood sucking fiends and leach madness." *SFGate,* 23 March 2003. https://www.sfgate.com/travel/departures/article/gory-story-of-bloodsucking-fiends-and-leech-2660739.
21 Covey, Stephen. 2020. "Circle of Influence v Circle of control." *Discovery In Action,* 4 Aug. 2020. https://discoveryinaction.com.au/circle-of-concern-v-circle-of-control.

22. Centerstone.org. 2023. "'How to Forgive Yourself & Let Go of Regrets - Centerstone.'" Centerstone. May 9, 2023. https://www.centerstone.org/our-resources/health-wellness/how-to-forgive-yourself-and-let-go-of-regrets.
23. Cuncic, Arlin, MA. 2023. "The Psychology of Shame." *Verywellmind*, 28 June 2023. https://www.verywellmind.com/what-is-shame-5115076.
24. "What Is Toxic Shame?" 2021. WebMD. March 31, 2021. https://www.webmd.com/mental-health/what-is-toxic-shame#:~:text=Toxic%20shame%20is%20a%20feeling,into%20a%20belief%20about%20yourself.
25. Tenth Avenue North. "You Are More." Track 3 on *The Light Meets the Dark*. Provident Label Group, 2010, CD.

Chapter 7

26. Guiness World Records
    a. Suggitt, Connie. 2021. "56-year-old freediver holds breath for almost 25 minutes breaking record." *Guinness World Records*, 12 May 2021. https://www.guinnessworldrecords.com/news/2021/5/freediver-holds-breath-for-almost-25-minutes-breaking-record-660285.
    b. "Longest Survival without Food." 1966. Guinness World Records. July 1, 1966. https://www.guinnessworldrecords.com/world-records/78789-longest-survival-without-food.
    c. Atwal, Sanj. 2023. "What's the limit to how long a human can stay awake? And why we don't monitor the record." *Guinness World Records*, 17 January 2023. https://www.guinnessworldrecords.com/news/2023/1/whats-the-limit-to-how-long-a-human-can-stay-awake-733188.
27. McLoed, Saul. 2023. "Maslow's Hierarchy of Needs." *Simple Psychology,* 26 July, 2023. https://www.simplypsychology.org/maslow.html.
28. Bethel Music. "God Of Revival." Track 1 on *Revival's In The Air*. Bethel Music Publishing, 2020, CD.
29. Owens, Ginny. "If You Want Me To." Track 5 on *Without Condition*. Rocketown Records, 1999, CD.

Chapter 8

30. LaFauci, Deana. 2022. "Tara Lipinski on the discipline to be great. Key Insights From Game Changers with Molly Fletcher." *Linkage,* 22 Feb. 2022. https://www.linkageinc.com/leadership-insights/tara-lipinski-on-the-discipline-to-be-great-key-insights-from-game-changers-with-molly-fletcher.
31. Gleeson, Brent. 2020. "9 Powerful Ways To Cultivate Extreme Self-Discipline." *Forbes,* 25 Aug. 2020. https://www.forbes.com/sites/brentgleeson/2020/08/25/8-powerful-ways-to-cultivate-extreme-self-discipline.

32 Miller, Rick. 2014. "The 5 Elements of Effective Leadership." *Being Chief,* 8 Sept. 2014. https://*www*.Beingchief.com/five-elements-effective-leadership.
33 Meyers, Rick. "Guzik's Commentary: Hebrews 12:1-29." e-Sword Bible app. Version 13.0.0.
34 Nordeman, Nichole. "The Unmaking." Track 1 on *The Unmaking.* Sparrow Records, 2015, CD.

Chapter 9

35 Hillsong United. "Know You Will." Track 11 on *Are We There Yet.* Hillsong Music and Resources, 2022, CD.

Chapter 10

36 EncourageTV. 2019. "Music Machine | Full Episode." https://www.youtube.com/watch?v=o_D67IOdqR0.
37 Stone, Jim. 2014. "The 7 Laws of Impatience." *Psychology Today,* 19 Nov. 2014. https://www.psychologytoday.com/us/blog/clear-organized-and-motivated/201411/the-7-laws-impatience.
38 Llerena, Katiah. 2017. "How to Cope With Impatience." *Gramercy Psychological Services,* 19 June 2017. https://www.Gramercypsychologicalservices.com/2017/06/19/how-to-cope-with-impatience/.
39 McConaughey, Matthew. 2020. "Greenlights." Crown Publishing.
40 Meyers, Rick. "Guzik's Commentary: Nehemiah 1:1-11." e-Sword Bible app. Version 13.0.0.
41 Shane & Shane. "I Will Wait For You (Psalm 130)." Track 7 on *Hymns Live.* Well House Records, 2019, CD.

Chapter 11

42 Pilastro, Eleonora. 2022. "Kate Jayden breaks record running 106 marathons in 106 days." *Guinness World Records,* 9 August 2022. https://www.guinnessworldrecords.com/news/2022/8/kate-jayden-breaks-record-running-106-marathons-in-106-days-712556.
43 Young, Brandon. 2020. "Perseverance is greater than Endurance: 5 factors of perseverance in adversity." *Thrive Global,* 16 Sept. 2020. https://community.thriveglobal.com/perseverance-is-greater-than-endurance-5-factors-of-perseverance-in-adversity/.
44 Fuller, Ben. "Who I Am." Track 2 on *Who I Am.* Provident Label Group, 2022, CD.

Chapter 12

45 Newman, Stephen M. 2022. "Nine expressions of Worship." *Experiencing Worship*, 7 April 2022. https://www.experiencingworship.com/articles/general/2001-6-nine-expressions-of-worship.

46 Maher, Matt. "Lord, I Need You." Track 4 on *All The People Said Amen*. Provident Label Group, 2013, CD.

Chapter 13

47 Nix, Elizabeth. 2015. "What was the 'shot heard round the world.'" *History*, 23 Jan. 2015. https://www.history.com/news/what-was-the-shot-heard-round-the-world.

48 Lowe, Debbie. 2020. "'Freedom is Not Free.'" *Carroll County Comet*, 27 May 2020. https://CarrollCountyComet.com/articles/freedom-is-not-free.

49 Powell, Mac. "New Creation." Track 2 on *New Creation*. Mac Powell Records, under exclusive license to Capitol CMG, 2021, CD.

Chapter 14

50 "Easter." n.d. USCCB. https://www.usccb.org/prayer-worship/liturgical-year/easter.

51 Elevation Worship. "Resurrecting." Track 5 on *Here As In Heaven*. Provident Label Group, 2016, CD.